WHAT IT *REALLY* TAKES TO GET INTO IVY LEAGUE & OTHER HIGHLY SELECTIVE COLLEGES

WHAT IT *REALLY* TAKES TO GET INTO IVY LEAGUE & OTHER HIGHLY SELECTIVE COLLEGES

CHUCK HUGHES

FORMER SENIOR ADMISSIONS OFFICER
HARVARD COLLEGE

McGraw-Hill

NEW YORK   CHICAGO   SAN FRANCISCO   LISBON   LONDON
MADRID   MEXICO CITY   MILAN   NEW DELHI   SAN JUAN   SEOUL
SINGAPORE   SYDNEY   TORONTO

3 4 5 6 7 8 9 0   AGM/AGM   0 9 8 7 6 5 4

ISBN 0-07-141259-X

McGraw-Hill books are available at special quantity discounts to use as premiums and sales promotions, or for use in corporate training programs. For more information, please write to the Director of Special Sales, Professional Publishing, McGraw-Hill, Two Penn Plaza, New York, NY 10121-2298. Or contact your local bookstore.

 This book is printed on recycled, acid-free paper containing a minimum of 50% recycled, de-inked fiber.

Library of Congress Cataloging-in-Publication Data

Hughes, Chuck (Chuck W.)
   What it really takes to get into the Ivy League & other highly selective colleges / Chuck Hughes.
      p. cm.
Includes bibliographical references and index.
   ISBN 0-07-141259-X (alk. paper)
   1. Universities and colleges—United States Admission—Handbooks, manuals, etc. I. Title.
   LB2351.2.H85 2003
   378.1'61'0973—dc21   2002155765

CONTENTS

ACKNOWLEDGMENTS

This book would not have been possible without the support from so many colleagues, past and present, friends, and family. My parents are the foundations of this book, as they have shaped who I am. Their commitment to providing for me and my sister the college educations that they never had has always been inspiring. Thanks to Catholic Memorial High School for helping me to develop my talents. From the admissions office to the athletic department, Harvard University is a place that I will forever "bleed crimson," and I am grateful for my nine years at Harvard as student and employee and to all those who have impacted me!

Thanks to Bill Fitzsimmons and Marlyn McGrath Lewis, who provided counsel and support during the revisions and drafting process. A great deal of credit has to go to my friend, former Harvard admissions office colleague and fellow Harvard alumnus Dan Drummond, who copyedited most of the book from his admissions/high school counseling perspectives. Thanks to Brother Andrew Prendergast for his valuable insights, to Norma Mushkat for putting the final touches on the copy for McGraw-Hill, and to Doug Hardy for guiding me through the writing and business perspectives on getting published. My close friend Peter Blacklow was instrumental, giving me the keys to his summer place in Falmouth during the fall and winter months for writing retreats, and for referring me to Howard Cohl, who did a phenomenal job as my book agent.

ACKNOWLEDGMENTS

Thanks to all of the students whom I advised at Harvard—on-campus advising is the best teaching tool for a young admissions officer! In particular, I want to thank the five students who were willing to be case studies in the book. Their willingness to share their stories with the public demonstrates the personal character that helped them to distinguish themselves as applicants and will lead them to tremendous successes in life.

The biggest thank-you goes to my wife Melissa, who was patient, encouraging, and supportive throughout this entire experience which has taken two-plus years to complete. She is my best friend, the love of my life, and has made the past six years most exciting.

A final acknowledgment goes to a poster that my father hung in our kitchen from the time I was eight years old until well after I graduated from Harvard in 1992. The poster portrayed a ballerina in dance and sums up the underlying message of this book and how I try to live my life:

If you imagine it, you can achieve it. If you dream it, you can become it.

Chuck Hughes

INTRODUCTION

Gaining admission to the nation's most highly selective colleges is one of the most competitive yet least understood processes in education today. The value placed upon receiving a prestigious university education over the past decade has increased dramatically, and more students are looking to attend the country's elite universities. At the same time, the appeal and reach of the Ivy League has broadened, attracting outstanding international students from all over the globe. The globalization of America's elite colleges has only made the admissions process more competitive. With such incredible competition and growth in the number of applications, parents and students need a resource to guide them through the inevitably nerve-wracking, intense admissions process that begins in earnest during senior year of high school. This book will do that while providing insights into what admissions offices look for in prospective college students.

What does it *really* take to get admitted to an Ivy League or other top college or university?

While there's no single path to becoming a compelling candidate for admission, the choices that high school students, parents, and guidance counselors make during the course of high school have a significant bearing on the admissions outcome. This book is designed to provide a comprehensive, easy-to-understand guide that outlines important criteria to consider when making choices, and it discusses how these choices might impact a candidate's chances for admission at highly selective colleges and universities.

For some, the above question about getting into a top college or university might be, "Am I a good enough candidate to even consider applying?" For many students, the answer is yes. But which school(s) will say yes to you? Once all the admissions offers have been doled out, choosing which school to attend is a little easier if you've done some research and determined in advance which schools are a good fit for you. Finding the best match for your interests, skills, and personality is every bit as important as determining where your chances for admission are highest.

This book will give you a better understanding of what it takes to become a stronger candidate in the competitive process of getting into a top school, as well as examine what goes into making a college or university a good fit for various applicants. We'll outline some of the key elements in the process—from the perspective of a former Harvard senior admissions officer—and offer insights on how students can effect change in their candidacy by making wise and timely decisions beforehand, and by improving their credentials in a relevant and strategic manner.

An Insider's Perspective

Before writing this book I asked myself three important questions to be certain it would be worthwhile for those students who faced the admissions process, as well as for their parents and guidance counselors.

What Makes Me an Expert? I spent five years as a senior admissions officer at Harvard College, and during three of those years I lived on campus as a proctor—a residential adviser to first year students. This afforded me the opportunity to see firsthand how the students we admitted adjusted to college, how they performed academically, and what impact they made on extracurricular life. Further, these experiences gave me a better understanding of how a student's high school contributions might translate in college after he or she has been admitted.

For an admissions officer, how a student might develop academically and socially during college is an important factor to consider during the evaluation process, when schools try and assess the fit between the candidate and the school. Understanding how students with certain credentials, backgrounds, and skills will perform on campus is clearly a valuable tool to have, one that I appreciated. Watching students grow in college, and considering that growth in the context of their applications and college experience, made me a much better judge of the next class of applicants. It also helped that I'd graduated from Harvard College myself, in 1992. My understanding of the school's values thus derived from being a student, an administrator, and an adviser.

How Does This Book Differ from Other Sources? I believe that by taking a holistic approach to explaining the process, and by providing suggestive tips on how to better prepare for the process, this book does indeed present a fresh and positive perspective on college admissions. The "holistic" approach means that we consider the world in which we live—with its human interactions, sociological influences, and political elements—when considering factors that play a significant role in admissions. The insights into what admissions staffs emphasize come from the same realistic context, with specific examples of what does and does not impress a staff.

Part I, What Matters to Admissions Offices, outlines key areas that are considered by admissions staffs: academic credentials, extracurricular activities, personal qualities, and other influencing factors. Part II, Understanding the Admissions Cycle, broaches the subject of how admissions officers rate applications, and examines the essential elements needed to build a strong admissions case. You'll no doubt also find it helpful to glimpse at what occurs behind the closed doors of admissions committee meetings and to learn more about who reads the applications and how the applications are presented.

The best way to gain an understanding of what it takes to be admitted to the most selective schools is to learn more about the individuals who've been admitted to these colleges. The anecdotal evidence drawn from past applicants often provides excellent examples of the issues and challenges admissions officers face when reviewing thousands of candidates, and we site these examples throughout the book.

Part III, Harvard Case Studies, particularly distinguishes this book from others on college admissions. From the viewpoint of an admissions officer, it examines five students who were admitted to Harvard College and attended the College between 1996 and 2003. Using the case-study methodology, these students' applications are evaluated in a format similar to the one in place when they initially applied and were reviewed during the admissions process.

Will This Book Help? My third question, when considering whether to write this book, was whether it would be helpful to students or parents who were considering highly selective colleges and universities. Those students, parents, and high school counselors interested in learning more about the process were my focus, and my challenge. Would they benefit from knowing the components of the process? And the answer was yes, that knowledge could significantly improve the chances for admission.

However, those who expect to find a secret formula to help gain entrance through the Ivy gates will find this book disappointing. The book was not written to expose a loophole in the process or provide a formula that guarantees success. If finding corners to cut were possible, revealing the "insider secrets" would have been bottled and sold to the masses long ago. What this book does, however, is give individual students the tools to become stronger candidates in the applicant pool. By understanding the critical elements in the process, following some high-level recommendations, and staying on top of the process, you or the students you work with will have the tools to create compelling admissions cases for any selective institution.

Complexities in the Admissions Process

Selective college admission is one of the most complicated and least understood processes within higher education. The process is both quantitative and qualitative—in the tools and methods used for assessing and ultimately selecting from among the world's top candidates. The flexible and dynamic nature of admissions at the nation's top schools, however, makes it difficult for counselors, parents, and students to apply the same general formula to every highly selective admissions group.

Despite the ambiguity, we aim to clarify and highlight the general and tangible credentials, characteristics, and criteria that the nation's top undergraduate institutions are seeking. Grades and test scores are only two areas that are quantified in the process. There are also important intangible strengths needed in an application to make the most compelling case. For example, how an applicant has responded to adversity may be evaluated. As you read the book, you'll gain insight not only into the qualifications and criteria that determine who gets admitted to the nation's top schools, but an appreciation for the "intangibles" that admissions officers evaluate and how your intangible assets can improve your candidacy.

There are so many different ways to look at college admissions that it can be difficult for those at a distance to grasp the nuances that contribute to the decision-making process. But you can simplify the process by focusing on those aspects over which you have the greatest control and influence. To that end, we will segment and highlight the critical components in an easily understood manner, while offering tips and guidance along the way to help you plan a strategy and think about what you're missing, and to give you the edge in your preparation, help bolster your credentials, and enhance your application. While finding a panacea that will produce certain admission to the school of your choice is highly unlikely, implementing some of the suggestions in this book will help prepare a candidate for the application process.

Whether you're interested in learning more about how to make your high school experiences count, or you want to know some of the dos and don'ts, or even if you would simply like a better appreciation of what university admissions offices take into account when evaluating candidates, this book will lay the foundation for understanding the admissions process. Also, understanding the human side of admissions and the most critical components for developing a strong candidacy will enable you to conduct a better self-assessment of your skills, and ultimately be better equipped to change, if necessary. This benefit will extend beyond becoming a better candidate for the most selective colleges—it can facilitate real personal growth and maturation, and that will pay direct dividends to students once they begin their college experience, no matter which schools accept them.

My five years at Harvard as an admissions officer has influenced much of my focus in this book on that institution. However, I also address many facets of the admissions process at all of the Ivy League schools: Brown, Columbia, Cornell, Dartmouth, Harvard, Pennsylvania, Princeton, and Yale. But the examples and tips are applicable to more than Ivy League admissions. Although there are nuances within highly selective institutions' admissions procedures, there are common values, principles, and factors that are critical to all top-tier schools. We'll discuss what the 50 to 100 most selective admissions offices expect to see from an application, which should help students become more informed decision makers while they're in high school.

In the book, I generally use the terms "highly selective" or "selective" to refer to the top 25 to 100 schools across the country. These schools are deemed selective because of their prestige and their relatively low admissions acceptance rates. As you will see, however, the acceptance rates at the top colleges and universities in the United States vary greatly, which give us our first insight into a very simple assessment: The odds of getting in can increase or decrease simply based on the schools to which you choose to apply.

What happens in America's universities, and how that impacts on high schools, is felt elsewhere. State and federal governments and education policy are sensitive to admissions policies, and as nonprofit, tax-exempt institutions that receive federal funding, many universities and their admissions offices are open to scrutiny by legislative bodies. The judiciary system has also become heavily involved in recent years, as the court system has been busy considering the role of standardized testing and admissions practices, with regard to diversity recruiting and the situation of minority applicants. Finally, the media has increasingly focused on the interest in "getting into college," and the marketplace has jumped in with both feet, offering an array of products that generate hundreds of millions of dollars in annual spending.

Given this situation, the attention focused on the admissions process is not surprising. Knowledge of the process is a highly sought after commodity as students and parents prepare for applying to college. Utilize the helpful tips and inside information in this book to your advantage.

PART I

COLLEGE ADMISSIONS 101: WHAT MATTERS TO ADMISSIONS OFFICES

A 10,000 FOOT VIEW OF SELECTIVE ADMISSIONS

The Long Line to Admission

A sagelike colleague of mine had a knack for reading an audience and sensing a tense atmosphere when he was about to give a presentation on admissions to Harvard College. He lightened the mood by drawing a long line above a short line on the nearest board or easel and began:

> Imagine that the long line is all that is known about the admissions process.
> Then the short line is all that is understood about the admissions process.
>
> Imagine that the long line is all that is understood about the admissions process.

Then the short line is all that I understand about the
admissions process.

The long line is all that I understand about the process.
The short line is all that I'll be able to tell you about the
process.

The long line is what I will tell you about the process.
The short line is what you will comprehend about the process.

The long line is admission to Harvard.
The short line is your chance of getting admitted.

Every time he began a presentation this way, the audience responded with a hearty laugh and a relieved sigh.

The level of uncertainty about the application process generates
a tremendous amount of anxiety in parents and students alike. The
story has been my colleague's way of explaining to the audience that
it's hard to get admitted to the most selective schools in America,
but one should not let what is not understood and what cannot be
controlled limit a person's dreams of attending a selective college.

Because the selective schools' admissions process is so competitive and intimidating, trepidation leads some students and parents
to focus on the process rather than on the things they can control.
Other parents and students choose to approach the process with an
epic intensity that causes them to lose perspective on the college experience itself, and to redirect their energies to getting accepted by
a prestigious university instead of finding the right school to attend.

My colleague's usual opening presentation is more than an ice-
breaking story. It represents the competitiveness in the application
process at the most selective colleges. It's difficult for even strong
students to gain admission to these institutions, and there are many

more factors to understand than you might expect. But the complexity does not preclude preparing effectively for the parts of the process that remain in your control. Like the long line and short line metaphor, this book will help you better understand the selective college admissions process, and in turn, it will give you the tools you need to more effectively prepare for it.

Though it's tough to be admitted to the top schools, it's not impossible. In fact, when you consider the caliber of education they provide, some of the top colleges and universities offer admission to a relatively high percentage of the total applicant pool. Table 1-1 lists the admission rates of Ivy League and other top national universities.

You can see that some of the top institutions in the country admit *one out of every three or four applicants.* There are other notable elite institutions and an amazing group of terrific schools not listed in the chart with higher acceptance rates, and this is encouraging news. At the same time, these numbers reflect the fact that many students receive multiple letters of acceptances to these universities, thereby diminishing the total number of unique students who receive admissions offers to selective institutions.

The Ivy League admissions data for the high school graduating class of 2001 reveals that approximately 130,000 applications were received and about 24,000 letters of acceptance were delivered, a collective acceptance rate of approximately 18 percent. While some students will receive multiple letters of acceptance, upward of 16,000 individuals will be offered admissions to at least one Ivy school annually.

Admission to highly selective colleges is a competitive process, and unfortunately, too many students in the past few years have taken an analytical approach to solving the competitive challenges of selective admissions. Certainly, there is value in doing research

Table 1-1 *Selective School Admission Rates*

Ivy League Schools	Admit Rate for Class of 2003 Applicants	Selective Schools with Admit Rate < 25%	Admit Rate for Class of 2003 Applicants
Harvard	11%	Harvard	11%
Princeton	11%	Princeton	11%
Columbia	14%	US Military Academy	13%
Yale	16%	Columbia	14%
Brown	17%	Stanford	15%
Dartmouth	21%	US Naval Academy	15%
University of Pennsylvania	26%	Yale	16%
Cornell	33%	Brown	17%
		California Institute of Technology	18%
		MIT	19%
		Amherst	19%
		US Air Force Academy	20%
		Dartmouth	21%
		Swarthmore	22%
		Georgetown	23%
		Williams	23%

Source: "America's Best Colleges, 2001 Edition," *U.S. News & World Report*. This data was provided to the magazine by the institutions and represents the acceptance rates for the college graduating class of 2003.

into admissions standards, but I wonder about those to whom understanding the process becomes the end in itself. Avoid getting caught up in attempting to uncover what admissions officers expect in an application. Getting tangled deep in the weeds of the nuances of the admissions process will most likely lead to overlooking the real opportunities to affect change and develop the candidate's natural talents, which in fact is the key to strengthening an admissions case.

Getting into highly selective colleges depends, of course, on the competition and the number of applicants in any pool of candidates. The larger the applicant pool and the stronger the candidates who are applying, the more difficult it will be. Admitting students to the most selective universities is far from a formulaic science, and as a process managed by people, it has an unmistakably human element. To better understand the value of a process that is considered more art than science, it is important to understand the roles and missions of Ivy League institutions.

We live in a world that for the most part wants a standardized and tangible structure of judgment, with standards that align clearly defined inputs in order to yield a specific output or result. When it comes to colleges and universities, that output is a letter of admission. But the myriad factors to be weighed during the process makes it nearly impossible to develop a formula that can account for the evaluation of the various skills and the potentials of highly qualified individuals. That is the goal of the admissions committee's decision-making process, which, as noted above, guides its judgment with educational and philosophical missions of the school. And since there are more highly qualified candidates in selective college applicant pools than openings, meeting these goals each year has become ever more challenging.

The Admission Mission: Prepare Leaders for the Twenty-First Century

Read through any university's chronicles or admissions literature and you'll find a consistent message that emphasizes the university's mission and commitment to educating twenty-first-century leaders. At Cornell the mission and values statement embodies the vision of its founder, Ezra Cornell, as an institution that "fosters personal discovery and growth, nurtures scholarship and creativity across a broad range of common knowledge, and engages men and women from every segment of society in this quest."[1] Princeton's unofficial mantra has been: "In the Nation's Service and in the service of all Nations."

None of the nation's most selective schools could accomplish their missions without looking to their admissions departments to recognize the institutions' essence and direction. Admissions offices are the frontline mechanism for finding, recruiting, and matriculating the most qualified individuals to fulfill and help perpetuate these important missions.

Universities have always sought to admit talented individuals who embody the institution's philosophy and vision. In 1948, Harvard Provost Paul Buck traced Harvard's modern mission to serve society to the university's longest serving president, Charles Eliot (1869–1909):

> President Eliot struck a note in his inaugural address on October 19, 1869, when he said, "The College is intensely American in affection, and is intensely democratic in effort." In recent years we have deliberately sought to draw our students from all sections of the country, and all types of schools, and from all economic levels.[2]

President Eliot captured the qualities that admissions officers have sought to find in applicants for generations. Their task is to find exceptional intellectual promise, impressive leadership qualities, outstanding personality characteristics, and demonstrable talents in areas beyond the classroom. To accomplish this, admissions offices look at applicants as a microcosm of society, in the hopes of addressing Eliot's vision of a university.

Despite Ivy League institutions' long-defined missions, however, there is no simple, objective formula that all universities use when making admissions selections. The essential principles and long-standing visions of the various institutions make it impossible to paint an exact picture of the ideal candidate; there are so many iterations of the "best" candidate.

Admissions offices and leading universities evaluate a range of both quantitative and qualitative criteria. While some would like to narrowly define the nation's elite universities as solely research and academic centers focused purely on churning out the next wave of faculty members and research scientists, leading university administrators recognize the importance of a broadly interpreted definition of excellence when it comes to undergraduate admissions. Of course, unusual academic promise is an important component of a university's mission; however, the Ivy League schools would have never reached their recognized levels of prominence in education had they strictly defined leadership as solely a function of academic achievement.

A selective institution's desire to educate and train the most talented student body from all types of socioeconomic backgrounds is not a new phenomenon. Leading institutions have long wanted a student body that is a cross section of society, because some of the most important learning that occurs on campus happens outside the classroom. The learning that goes on outside of the classroom at highly selective universities is as distinguishing an aspect of one's college experience as the outstanding caliber of academic resources. Personally, what I learned from my peers at Harvard was every bit as valuable as my classroom education. When I was trying to make my decision on whether to attend Harvard, I remember my interviewer saying that most stimulating conversations and most memorable learning experiences would be just as likely to occur in the dining hall as they would in the lecture hall. With anywhere from 15,000 to 20,000 applicants in a given year applying for 1100 to 3000 seats, depending upon the Ivy League institution, admissions committees are faced with making difficult choices among talented applicants. It's not just the number of applicants, but the all-around strength and talents within Ivy League applicant pools that require an admissions committee to make fine distinctions among highly qualified applicants. Add the influence of a university's mission and its institutional goals, and the manner in which applicants are selected becomes more an art than a more formulaic science.

Universities Don't Just Admit Individuals— They Build Classes

Admissions offices are in the business of not only selecting individuals, but also of building classes. Building a class is similar to building a team, an orchestra, or any organization that is a sum of its parts. Similar to an orchestra that can't play a mellifluous symphony without a full suite of musicians and instruments, any university will have trouble perpetuating its mission if its admissions office is unable to build strong matriculating classes that impact as many aspects of campus life as possible. Class building is a painstakingly laborious art that combines selecting candidates with unique and outstanding talent with a collective broad and worldly view. Like the symphony orchestra, a class is the sum of its parts, a wide swath of interests, backgrounds, and viewpoints.

Admissions offices at Ivy League schools are tasked by and work with faculty to build the most dynamic class possible. Part of the responsibility that comes with building such a class is the expectation that individual admissions will be able to meet the institutional goals set at the beginning of each academic year with aplomb. Although these "institutional needs" may vary from campus to campus, deans of admission are constantly working with all members of the university community to achieve these goals.

The faculty committee on admissions attempts to identify significant areas of interest that admissions officers should make concerted efforts to attract and admit. For instance, they may need to recruit and admit more students within a particular academic focus, within a new degree program, and within an existing program that has seen a recent drop in enrollment. Or they may even need to recruit within an area that has recently received a capital commitment designed to improve the quality of education.

In addition to academic initiatives, the faculty committee, as well as university administrators and presidents, seek to support nonacademic areas of interest. Whatever the institutional goals set each year by the school, nearly all members within the university community—academic and nonacademic—are interested in bringing more students into their area of expertise. Throughout the year, departmental faculty, administrators, alumni office members, coaches, and the like spend considerable time lobbying the admissions staff to push for outstanding candidates in the areas they serve. If a school is placing a particular emphasis on a degree program or some other initiative in a given year and you possess the requisite skills, you're likely to find yourself to be a particularly compelling candidate.

During my five years in admissions, plenty of faculty members told me that we needed to admit more history majors, more chemistry students, more classics majors, more students whose interest was in engineering. Imagine the challenge admissions offices must face when they seek to find candidates who can complete the requirements, potentially excel in that major in college, and then choose to graduate with a major in the field that he or she indicated an interest in studying as a high school senior.

Many schools also have a strong interest in actively supporting the recruitment of women in higher education. For example, all universities compete to attract the top women interested in engineering, mathematics, and the physical sciences, since traditionally fewer women have had the opportunity to study, or shown an interest in studying, these disciplines. Knowing the academic recruiting goals of a department can be a real strategic advantage for an applicant. It can help you to identify where your academic interests might be a particularly strong match with the university's direction and emphasis. Recruiting initiatives in admissions are also strong indicators that these academic disciplines will receive a solid commitment from the university administration during your enrollment period.

At some schools, it is a taxing endeavor for admissions officers when choices have to be made between engineers, classicists, and mathematicians, given the high interest level from faculty members. Admissions offices will do everything they can to admit qualified candidates genuinely interested in studying lesser subscribed programs. At other schools, a dearth of applicants interested in studying in a particular area that has been given a recruiting priority may bode well for those in the applicant pool. It follows that it's important that the applicant know the institution's academic makeup and its focus on admitting students interested in specific disciplines.

TIP: *Be sure to research schools that focus their marketing efforts on areas of study that match your academic interests. They may be looking to increase enrollments in these majors.*

Nonacademic institutional needs are also actively supported at all universities, though at varying levels. University administrators in nonacademic life also lobby the admissions offices to admit more candidates interested in an array of social, cultural, and extracurricular activities. The music or orchestra director might advocate for more cellists in a given year, while the athletic director might stress the role of athletics within the university and even highlight a handful of programs for emphasis. Others may advocate for greater socioeconomic, cultural, religious, or ethnic diversity on campus, depending upon their role within the university.

Many institutions care about their relationship with local and state communities and its impact on the long-term success of the institution. As nonprofit institutions, universities have to maintain strong relationships with the communities that will politically shape their future. Cambridge and Boston are closely partnered with Harvard. The University of Pennsylvania and Philadelphia have close ties. The relationship between New Haven and Yale has strengthened. The involvement of these three and many other universities with their local communities is also significant.

On the state level, a higher proportion of students are generally admitted from the school's home state than are admitted from other states. This makes sense since these residents are more likely to become future local and state politicians and policy makers. University relationships with the towns and cities where the school resides are also important. The admissions offices at these schools take great care to admit strong candidates from these communities, but moving to New Haven for your senior year in high school will not increase your admissions chances at Yale. At the same time as they're aware of the local community and state concerns, the most highly selective institutions also want to be national and global leaders. In the last five years several Ivy League schools have been typical in this regard by making significant commitments to recruit top talent from around the world. At Penn, nearly 10 percent of the class of 2003 was schooled abroad, while at Brown and Cornell the figures are 9 and 9.5 percent respectively.

With so many different interests from so many different corners of the university, it becomes important for the dean or the director of the admissions office to keep one eye on the big picture at a 10,000-foot level as the admissions committee looks at individuals and the contributions that each candidate can make to that larger class on a case-by-case basis.

Individual Assessment: The Key Criteria

The balance between building a class and admitting individual candidates each year becomes the true challenge for an admissions staff. Knowing the school's goals, focus, and needs, staff members delve into the applications and begin reading and learning about the candidates. Highly selective schools are searching for accomplishment, leadership, and achievement. Demonstrable talents manifest themselves in many ways, but admissions officers are trained to find these talents by looking at four broad areas:

- Academic achievement

- Extracurricular activities

- Personal qualities

- Intangible and other influencing factors

All four of these criteria build a case that helps a committee make difficult choices among the incredibly well-qualified candidates. Rarely does a student gain admission to the most selective schools without excelling in more than one of the four areas. For those whose talents may shine exceedingly bright in one area and less so in others, their admission will hinge on just how bright that light shines in that sphere. These candidates are likely to be in the top 1 percent nationally in their specialty. But even in these cases, the personal traits of candidates are important. Although such qualities and other intangible factors are the most qualitative and subjective, they help fill in the missing pieces of an application. They can often tip the scales one way or the other when admissions officers are trying to sift through information about highly qualified applicants, only a small percentage of whom can be accepted.

In addition to all of the points we've so far touched upon, one of the main reasons admissions offices are looking for multitalented candidates who can excel in several areas is because there are so many great candidates. Each year, more qualified candidates are in the applicant pool than there are available spaces. Admissions offices estimate that 80 to 85 percent of the applicants could handle the academic workload at the most selective schools. I would add that 40 percent of the applicants would be great choices at any of the colleges. At the end of the process each year, we would look back at the class that had most recently been admitted and wish there had been another 500 to 1000 spaces available to offer those candidates who were just on the other side of the admissions fence.

Over the next several chapters we will consider the four prominent areas that contribute to the admissions decision-making process. As the pieces come together, a potential applicant will better comprehend the thought processes of admissions officers and the subsequent choices they make.

To get the most out of this analysis, you should evaluate each section by assessing the key criteria discussed within the section, and meanwhile ask yourself what other factors—beyond the scope of those criteria—might enhance or limit that particular activity, accomplishment, or circumstance within a full application. Of course, we'll go into this in more detail.

There are also many anecdotal applicant cases mentioned throughout the book that present examples of candidates whose profiles reflect the positive and sometimes negative factors that impact admissions decision making. Understanding the parts weighed in the process and how one's accomplishments will have an impact, the candidate will be able to present his or her strengths more persuasively in the application and, ultimately, improve the chances for admission.

Endnotes

1. "Cornell's Mission and Values," Cornell University Web site, www.info.cornell.edu/CUHomePage/Mission.html, March 15, 2002.

2. Paul Buck, "Who Comes to Harvard?" *Harvard Alumni Bulletin*, January 10, 1948.

ACADEMIC ASSESSMENT: ARE GOOD GRADES AND STRONG SAT SCORES ENOUGH?

Most of the students who apply to top universities are more than capable academically. The average candidate has strong grades, is among the top 10 percent in their class, and has solid to excellent SAT or ACT test scores. So what scores, grade point average, and class rank is enough to impress selective admissions offices?

At the simplest level, a well-rounded academic portfolio of more than 1400 on the SAT I and SAT II scores as well as a strong grade point average (GPA) that places the candidate in the top 5 to 10 percent of the high school class positions a candidate as a solid academic contender. But so many students apply to highly selective universities today with these credentials that we have to go beyond impressive scores and placements and understand the expectations of admissions officers as they assess these academic credentials. Among the many factors an admissions officer considers when trying to forecast a candidate's academic and intellectual promise, three stand out:

1. Academic rigor, GPA, and class rank

2. Standardized test scores

3. Academic awards, research, and other notable accomplishments

Analyzing Academic Rigor, GPA, and Class Rank

In evaluating an application at an Ivy League school, experienced admissions officers usually begin by examining the rigor of the student's academic workload. It doesn't take very long to recognize whether an applicant is challenging himself or underachieving. Admissions officers work hard at getting to know the schools for which they are assigned to read applications, and they become familiar with the levels of academic challenge those high schools offer. They read the school profiles, compare the course loads between students, and regularly call high school counselors to ask about classes and grades. In particular, high school counselors are asked to indicate whether an applicant is taking the most demanding, very demanding, demanding, average, or below average curriculum—a quick indicator of the commitment an applicant has to his or her studies.

The level of rigor indicates as much about the candidate's willingness to work as the candidate's ability level. Almost all the students admitted to elite colleges will have taken a first (most demanding) or second tier (very demanding) academic program. Even at the "very demanding" level of intensity, questions may arise as to why the applicant is not taking a more challenging academic program, leading an admissions staff to wonder if the student is prepared for the academic demands of a university education. Students interested in clearing this basic yet substantial hurdle in the admissions process should be taking as many of the most demanding courses available as possible. For those who have not taken as challenging a program as possible, it might be helpful for their counselors to highlight why alternative academic options were chosen.

At the same time, there is flexibility in terms of what constitutes a challenging curriculum. Students who attend small or poor schools with limited college preparatory offerings are not penalized because they haven't had the opportunity to take advanced coursework, and students who attend large suburban or magnet schools are not mandated to take every Advanced Placement (AP) or International Baccalaureate (IB) course offered. Schedule conflicts or extracurricular responsibilities may have necessitated a lower level of rigor, so admissions officers will evaluate rigor in the context of how these choices compare to the schedules of other students at the school.

I was always impressed with a student who prepared early enough to have taken all the AP classes their high school offered, but I did not differentiate that candidate from others at the same school who took four Advanced Placement classes instead of six. At the extremes, the fact that a student only takes one or two APs when the school offers 12 to 15 courses will certainly raise questions from admissions officers, as will the student who did not take any of the four AP classes offered at a less comprehensive school. The AP program offers upward of 35 AP exams, and the list is growing. But students should not feel pressured to take an inordinate number of APs, particularly if these courses are limiting one's personal growth in other areas. It's okay during senior year to take three AP exams instead of four, or two instead of three, especially if the student's energy is expended productively elsewhere.

The same holds true for International Baccalaureate Diploma programs, popular in Florida and Texas high schools. Students must select courses that are a good match, since they will need to balance Subsidiary Level (SL) and Higher Level (HL) course offerings. The additional component to consider for students who attend IB schools, however, is that selective universities give extra weight to students who complete the requirements needed to receive the full IB diploma. Because the diploma requirements include an extended essay and community service work in addition to successful completion of the HL courses, the intensive two-year program is highly regarded as an internationally rigorous course of study.

Academic and Extracurricular Balance

While it's important to take challenging courses in high school, two factors outside the academic context need to be considered to determine whether a student's schedule limits the potential for personal growth and development beyond the classroom.

First, is the student setting herself up for admissions failure? Taking a killer academic schedule is sound strategy, but students aren't doing themselves a favor if the result is poor grades in some or all of their classes because they are so consumed with studying 24/7 and begin to burn out.

Second, are school studies taking away from a student's ability to participate in activities outside of the classroom? It is important to maintain solid school-life balance. Engaging in fulfilling and relevant experiences outside the class environment not only adds to the substance of an application, but it adds a personal perspective that is an invaluable part of the maturation process. Although we'll talk more about extracurricular activities later, the large majority of students admitted to the most selective schools find time to contribute meaningfully to communities beyond the classroom.

> **TIP:** *Take a rigorous academic program, but be sure to create the best environment to succeed and avoid academic burnout.*

Extenuating Circumstances

In addition to understanding the course offerings of a particular high school, a good admissions officer will even become familiar enough with a school to know which teachers are the most demanding. Knowing a school at this level can be very helpful when clarifying information that might otherwise be devastating for an applicant. For example, I had an applicant apply through the *Early Action* program[1] with a very strong case for admission. He attended a reputable private school in the Boston area, was the school's extracurricular leader, was ranked third in the class, and had strong test scores and an interest in foreign languages.

The case looked like a sure early admit, until the first-term grades came in with a C+ in Calculus, the only C on his transcript in almost three and a half years of high school. After calling the school, it turned out that the teacher was notorious for hitting seniors with tough grades. Of the dozen or so students in the class, no one had received a grade above B in the first term. The school gave strong support to the candidate, and informed us that his second-term grade had risen to a B/B+ level, among the top grades in the class. Given his strong leadership in drama and other school programs, his outstanding references from his school and his alumni interview, and his otherwise excellent transcript, the student was ultimately offered an early admissions spot.

We will discuss the value of the high school counselor later in the book, but this is a good example of how counseling can make a difference in an admissions case. The counselor was positive about the candidate, and proactive in getting a statement from the teacher and providing us with the last-minute grades prior to the final Early Action meetings in the beginning of December. Students who receive a grade that is an aberration on an otherwise strong transcript may become candidates whose admissions hinge on late information that mitigates the questions the grade raises. A positive call from the counselor or a letter from the teacher can be a proactive way for the school to advocate on behalf of a student whose difficult subject matter or personal hardships might explain temporary academic struggles. It's more likely that an admissions office will contact the school if it's looking for more details, but an endorsement of the candidate will never hurt the applicant's chances.

Evaluating Grades

Evaluating grades is not the most challenging job of an admissions officer, but in an era of grade inflation, grades must be taken into account with the rigor of the program and the school's grading style.

A low B grade may not mean the same thing at many of the affluent suburban and private school communities that it did 15 or 20 years ago. At one outstanding public high school in Seattle, teachers did not give B's to students in top tier programs, and most of the transcripts I read were straight A transcripts. Students ranked as low 30th in the class would have a straight A record, and it was uncommon to see more than one or two B's on the transcript.

Grade inflation at public schools in many states has evolved to help more students receive automatic admission to certain in-state universities, and also in response to parental and community pressure to reward hardworking students with better grades. At some private schools, teachers are hesitant to give grades below the B range for fear of harming the academic record of a student who will most likely apply to a selective school of some sort. At least two private schools in Massachusetts that I know about were notorious for not giving grades below a B–. Students ranked in the bottom 40 percent of the class at these schools still had averages from 82 to 84, and few if any grades in the C range.

It would be great if an A meant the same thing at every school across the country, but with the increasing pressures parents, school systems, politicians, and others have placed on secondary schools, that kind of standardization is unlikely. Thus, distinguishing the subtleties within grade ranges at specific schools has become the burden of admissions officers. For secondary schools that send a regular flow of applications to selective colleges, a candidate's level of achievement for that high school is not hard to recognize. Schools that employ too much grade inflation, however, run the risk of diminishing the importance of the high grades given to their students, at least when it comes to the application process. Admissions officers will weigh other quantitative data such as class rank and standardized test scores when the significance of the grades are diminished by inflation.

Students often asked me if I'd rather see a student get a B in an AP class or get an A in an honors course. Like many admissions professionals, my sardonic response was always, "Get an A in the AP class." I would follow the quip with a smile and explain that colleges want to see students perform at the highest levels possible. If that meant getting a few B's in AP courses, I would prefer those results every time; however, if modest results were also cutting into your extracurricular time as a musician or a debater, then I might recommend finding a different academic balance.

A light academic schedule is always noticed in the admissions process. High school counselors are asked to indicate the student's level of rigor, and a listing of the top courses offered is often provided by the school in a high school profile attached to the application. From this, admissions officers could compare the programs among candidates from the same school. I never had a problem with students at the same school having different programs and interests, but I was always concerned with a significant difference in the course load and rigor among those candidates.

Trends in a Transcript

Admissions officers also look at trends in the transcript. A "rising record" can boost a case that is on the edge. An upward trend might be a sign of maturity or an indication that the candidate is coming into his or her own. A "falling record," on the other hand, is an ominous flag in the admissions world. Immediately, readers and staffers begin to question the candidate's performance. Has the student hit a period of adversity? Has the student begun "senior slide" a bit too soon? Have the more challenging courses brought about a regression and thus revealed an applicant's true capabilities? Is it an indication of other personal problems that may negatively manifest themselves in college?

Admissions offices would much rather see steady improvement from a candidate than uneven performance or, of course, a marked downward trend. A sliding record without an explanation can be fatal for an applicant. Keep in mind that the fall semester of senior year is the last opportunity to provide an admissions office with a full academic update. In addition to one last set of semester grades, most high schools recalculate class rank at semester's end, which can have an impact on one's admission.

TIP: *Stay focused senior year! A sub par semester can be devastating, while a strong first term can boost rank and is expected from highly selective admissions offices.*

Class Rank

Finally, class rank is tied to the grades and rigor, and is an important part of evaluation. The class ranking is valuable because it provides some level of student comparison within the school. Admissions offices are less concerned with absolute class rank than in detailed and valid tools to help determine who the top scholars are within the school. Percentile ranking, grade distribution graphing, and GPA scatter plotting help them conduct accurate assessments of a student's academic performance.

Absolute rank has lost some importance in the last few years because ranking policies have changed at many schools. It's reached the point where many students at certain schools share the position of valedictorian. For instance, out of 19 applicants to Harvard one year from the previously mentioned high school in Seattle 11 were ranked first in their class. Several other schools in the country produced 20, 30, or even more valedictorians, because rank was not weighted, but calculated solely by grade point average.

Many schools have moved away from providing any type of rank because school committees, under the pressure of parents and students, believe that class rank does not accurately portray the performance of their students or the rigor of their academic programs. While I understand these concerns, I can tell you that admissions offices will rank students within their applicant pools if the schools do not provide rank. At the other end of the ranking spectrum, many public schools have simply chosen to rank any student with a 4.0 as first in the class. This type of grade inflation is not only done to cluster top students together, but also because such ranking systems can place more students into higher percentile groupings and thus help them gain admission to prestigious state institutions. University systems in California or Texas, for example, offer every student who is ranked in the top 5 to 10 percent of their high school graduating class a place at the most prestigious schools within their system.

Admissions officers are looking for reasons to admit students, and it's harder for them to advocate on behalf of a candidate when the picture is muddled or incomplete. There are three good reasons to provide at least a percentile rank or a GPA distribution of the senior class in the school profile.

First, it makes a lot more sense for an admissions officer to get an accurate approximation of a student's rank from the school than it does to leave it to an admissions office to estimate rank at its own discretion.

Second, schools that do not rank—because they're looking to elevate a larger middle group of *Prairie Home Companion*–type children, who are "above average" but not necessarily the cream of that year's crop—can hurt the candidacy of the top two or three candidates in the class.

Third, class rank is an important marketing component and assessment tool for colleges. Whether it's imprinted in admissions publications or part of a "Best Colleges" report, class rank is a closely monitored and reported statistic. Rank in class is also a metric that admissions offices report to the faculty and to the university. Schools are cognizant of the number of valedictorians who apply and who are admitted, and they similarly track the numbers of students who are in the top 5 to 10 percent of their graduating class. This is a statistic admissions offices can use to help develop programs and strategies that improve the school's image and broaden its appeal. Several schools have focused on this area as a way to improve not only the statistical quality of a class, but also their rankings within media publications that weight class rank as a factor in evaluating school selectivity.

Standardized Testing

The SAT I

Standardized testing has become one of the most controversial topics in education today. Whether it's a discussion on the role of state standards for high school graduation or an analysis of the validity and fairness of tests like the SAT exams, educators are torn on the merits of such testing. Whatever the merits of the arguments on either side of the debate, it is important to have a better understanding of why the SAT I, the SAT II, and the ACT exams matter, though not in as strictly defined a manner as one might expect.

The SAT I has a long history in education. Created in 1926, it has been an examination tool used by the Ivy League to assess a candidate's academic preparation. For years, each of the Ivy schools offered their own entrance exams, but over time, the need for highly selective schools to offer one exam that could be administered nationally developed, and Ivy League schools came together to create the SAT. It was attractive to have an exam that might create a standard baseline from which candidates' core writing and math skills could be compared. Today, with over 22,000 high schools, a growing home-schooling trend, and an increasing international applicant pool, the need for a common measuring stick is as evident as when the SAT I exam was first created.

In addition, as secondary schools have begun to suppress rank and to inflate grades, admissions offices have had to turn to testing to clarify an academic picture that has become less clear. The SAT I, with all its flaws, has remained a constant for admissions professionals, and it continues to serve as a tool to compare candidates' academic credentials from across the world.

When taken in context with school, geographical, cultural, and socioeconomic factors, SAT I scores can be used as a barometer for a candidate's preparedness for the first year of academic life in college. The correlation between SAT scores and performance in college is enhanced when combined with high school grades and a student's level of rigor. According to a College Board study in 1999, SAT I scores had a 0.52 correlation, which means they explained 52 percent of the variance in freshman grades. When combined with high school grades, however, the correlation jumped to 0.61.[2] For those who are less statistically inclined, such as myself, this correlation tells us that freshman grades hypothetically correlate at a reasonably high level to high school grades and SAT I scores. However, taken out of this context, an SAT I score can tell us much less about a candidate's intellectual promise.

Understanding the wide range of SAT I scores for admitted students can also help prospective candidates evaluate the selectivity of top colleges. You'll find mid-50 percent SAT scores for the class of 2003 at Ivy League institutions in Figure 2-1.

Figure 2-1 clearly shows that one does not need to score 1600 to gain admission to the most selective schools in America, and that 25 percent of the students admitted to these schools have scores below the ranges some might consider Ivy League–type numbers. Twenty-five percent of Cornell's class of 2003—which in fact is about 800 students—have a best SAT I score below 1270. It's safe to say that many more than 800 of the roughly 6500 plus students admitted to Cornell for the class of 2003 also had SAT I scores below 1270. Stu-

Figure 2-1 *Ivy League Mid-50 Percent SAT I Test Range*

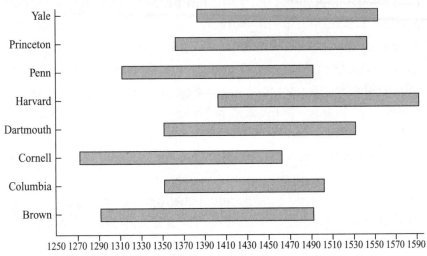

Source: *America's Best Colleges*, U.S. News & World Report, 2001.

dents admitted to highly selective colleges who have scored below mid-range most likely have a major hook—exceptional personal qualities or some other facet that makes them compelling candidates for admission. What I hope the graph illustrates is that highly selective universities do not rely solely on SAT I scores when evaluating candidates.

Another limiting factor on SAT I scores is the acknowledgment that these tests do not accurately predict future success. Lower test scores will not prohibit a person from becoming a successful businessperson, politician, or leader in society. In fact, our admissions office liked to allude to the fact that some of the most measurably successful alumni had SAT I scores in the bottom 25 percent of their class. In many instances, these alumni have experienced substantial financial success and become loyal financial donors to the institution.

Best-selling author Thomas Stanley's *The Mind of a Millionaire* supports the notion that the SAT I has little correlation to financial success. According to his survey of millionaires in the United States, the "average SAT I score of 1190 is significantly above the norm but not considered high enough to gain admittance to the so-called selective or competitive undergraduate colleges."[3] Like the millionaire Stanley depicts in his book, students with lower test scores who do gain admission to the most selective institutions have an unusual desire to succeed. They are focused, hardworking, and take advantage of opportunities available to them. We'll discuss this further when we look at the personal qualities and intangible factors needed to strengthen one's candidacy. For now, suffice it to say that these factors can help a student overcome any academic hurdle he or she might encounter in college.

Even if SAT I tests by themselves were an accurate predictor of academic performance, admissions offices would still have to consider other factors in the decision-making process because of the sheer number of applicants with high SAT I scores.

Let's consider a 1400 SAT I an outstanding result. In the college graduating class of 2002—consisting of seniors who graduated from high school in 1998—54,013 students scored 700 or higher on the verbal section (5 percent of all test takers), and 65,247 students scored 700 or higher on the math portion (6 percent of all test takers).[4] Just looking at these candidates, admissions offices would still receive more applicants than there are spaces available. At Harvard, among those who applied to the class of 2003, there were 8147 applicants with an SAT I Verbal score of 700 or better, and 9142 applicants who scored 700 or higher on the SAT I Math.[5] These test takers represented 48.5 and 54.4 percent of the applicant pool respectively, and about 35 percent of the pool scored a 700 on both the

SAT I Verbal and Math. Even if the most selective schools were to use this high-achieving threshold, there would still be many more candidates vying for admission with these testing credentials than there are available spaces.

Scores are important, but again, they have to be considered in context with one's high school grades, extracurricular activities, and personal qualities. Every year, numerous students with high scores on the SAT I exhibit poor academic performance and are not offered admission. In other cases, bright students with strong scores may lack the social skills and coping mechanisms necessary to handle the demands of living on their own in college dormitories. Consider the number of students who scored a perfect 800/800 SAT I in one sitting. For the class of 2003 throughout the country, 673 of all students who took the SAT I scored 1600, and approximately two-thirds of them applied to Harvard. Of these applicants, fewer than 200 were offered admission. To me, this is a telling sign that admissions officers are looking for more than just a sterling SAT I score.

Changes in Air for the SAT I. Over the past several years, confidence in the significance and relevance of SAT I as a tool for evaluating college applicants has eroded in many high schools and college admissions offices. In June 2002, in response to the needs of colleges and high schools, the College Board announced a comprehensive and sweeping overhaul of the SAT I. The new SAT I, to be implemented in March 2005, will focus more on reading comprehension and writing skills and less on analogy-type questions. The math portion of the SAT I will add Algebra II to the test and eliminate quantitative comparisons, in an effort to align the test more closely with high school curricula.[6]

While there may be significant changes in the way that the SAT of March 2005 will be evaluated, these changes will have no impact on the college admissions process for high school students who will graduate by June 2005. For the next two years, at least, little will change in the way in which high schools, parents, students, and colleges regard the present iteration of the SAT I. Teaching "to the tests" and paid SAT tutoring will continue to be common and accepted preparation practices.

The ACT Alternative

The ACT, another national college admissions entrance examination, has been a solid alternative/compliment to the SAT I examination at most competitive colleges. It consists of English, math, reading, and science reasoning examinations, and the results are individually scored as well as rolled into a composite test score.

Almost every institution offers applicants the choice between taking the ACT or the SAT I. Many highly selective schools will require one of these tests in addition to requiring three SAT II examinations. All of the Ivy League schools offer applicants the choice between submitting the ACT or the SAT I examination results and require three SAT II subject tests. Brown and Penn, however, allow the ACT to substitute for both the SAT I and the SAT II. Other schools, such as Stanford and the University of Chicago, do not require the SAT II and ask applicants to submit either ACT or the SAT I results. At nearly every selective institution, SAT II exams are strongly encouraged in addition to the ACT or SAT I exams, even if they are not required for admission.

One of the benefits in taking the ACT to the SAT is that ACT tests cover a broad, curriculum-based content. Many admissions offices value the subject exams and view testing based on classroom learning as a distinguishing feature from the SAT I. The Ivy League admissions offices have also created a conversion formula that translates the ACT score into an effective SAT I score for comparing students regardless of the examination selected. At Harvard, we typically compared the English ACT score to the SAT I Verbal, the ACT math score to the SAT I math score, and the ACT composite score to the SAT I combined score average. The conversion for comparing ACT results to SAT I results is listed in Table 2-1.

Table 2-1 *ACT/SAT Conversion Table*

ACT Score	SAT Conversion
15	370
16	400
17	420
18	440
19	460
20	480
21	500
22	520
23	540
24	560
25	570
26	590
27	610
28	630
29	650
30	670
31	690
32	710
33	740
34	760
35	780
36	800

A review of the formula reveals that the ACT score is multiplied by 20 and then an additional 70 or 80 points are added to the score to attain the converted score.

While the ACT offers some granularity in its assessments, for many admissions offices the tests do not have the same subject specificity as the SAT II exams or the Advance Placement tests. Schools that encourage applicants to take and submit SAT II exams should view that recommendation as a requirement and submit SAT II results as well.

> **TIP:** *Schools that specifically state in an application that SAT II are "encouraged" or "strongly encouraged" are essentially stating that neither the ACT nor the SAT I exam will suffice as standardized testing unless other significant academic data is provided—such as the SAT II, AP, or IB exam results.*

SAT II and the Value of Subject Specific Exams

As a senior admissions officer, I always placed a more significant value on SAT II tests because these exams are subject specific and can often be considered in context with an applicant's academic plans for college. Many of the highly selective schools require students to take the SAT II subject tests. The scores have a slightly higher correlation with one's performance in college than those of the SAT I.

The subject tests are a more predictable measure of performance because they are more closely aligned to college curricula than the SAT I. Also, SAT II results allow staffers to evaluate the student's "match" with his or her intended major. This is particularly valuable for colleges that require students to apply to specific schools, divisions, or colleges. For example, math and physics scores will be looked at closely for students interested in Engineering, Physics, or other physical science majors, while the Latin SAT II will become more important if Classics is a potential academic focus. High SAT II scores in chemistry and physics are much better predictors of one's ability to complete the degree requirements in a Chemical Engineering program than the SAT I math scores.

SAT I and SAT II scores are valuable because admissions officers can evaluate these scores in context with each applicant's intended major, and then try to assess how difficult the program might be for the candidate. A student who wants to be a doctor, for example, and has scored a 590 on the Biology SAT II, a 610 on the Math IIC, and a 560 on the chemistry exam is going to make a committee wary of her ability to make it through a premed program in college. The scores indicate that this student may have a hard time making it through a competitive college's premedical curriculum, and admissions offices try to minimize the chances for failure when they recognize a student's low probability for successfully completing the requirements. In this case, even if the applicant was accepted and manages to scrape through, poor academic performance as an undergraduate will make it more difficult to gain admission to graduate school. This too can be a factor in admissions decisions.

One of the measures to ascertain the academic "fit" of a candidate is his or her commitment to the degree program or graduate school area in.conjunction with the subject matter scores. A student with low math scores who is absolutely committed to becoming an actuary will be a less appealing candidate than one with the same interest in actuarial work and similar test scores but who indicates he is not committed to that program to the exclusion of all others. The second candidate shows flexibility, indicating to admissions officers that he will be more likely to move into another field that might produce better academic success.

Students should take SAT II exams in the areas for which they're interested in studying, since it will give the candidate and the admissions office more information about their preparedness for that degree program. A student who wants to be a French major should take the SAT II exam in French to demonstrate his facility in the subject matter to the admissions office. By not taking an exam in a primary field of interest, neither the students nor the institution will have an adequate understanding of whether that field might be a difficult major to pursue. Additionally, admissions officers may look more skeptically at applications that do not show the proper preparation demonstrated with a solid SAT II score when a test is offered in that area.

TIP: *Avoid selecting "absolutely certain" as a commitment level for a major if your SAT II scores in those areas are not in the high 600s or better.*

Several of the SAT II tests seemed to be producing more high scores than we'd anticipated at Harvard. Since the recentering of SAT I and SAT II scores in 1995, the SAT II exam in writing and the Math IIC exam produced a significantly greater number of 800 test scores than our office had previously seen. Although the 800 scores were proportionately given, based on performance and the number of test takers for a given test, the big numbers were viewed as less impressive because they were seen more frequently.

In 1995 only 32 students who applied to Harvard scored an 800 on the writing exam, and 90 scored an 800 on Math IIC. Since the recentering, approximately 600 applicants per year in the Harvard applicant pool have scored 800 in writing, and over 1500 applicants have received an 800 on the Math IIC. The dramatic jump took a little luster off the value of the score in these areas as we read through the applications.

In addition, the SAT II writing exam can produce some uneven scoring. Because the College Board hires different readers to grade the tests, there are occasions where the writing score seems to be disparate from the SAT I verbal score, other SAT II scores, and/or the personal essay. There were plenty of examples of applicants who had mediocre SAT I and other test scores, received a big SAT II writing score, and then produced an essay that was less than impressive to admissions officers.

SAT Test Preparation

I've tried to avoid the questions regarding bias and the validity of the SAT I. Organizations such as FairTest and, more recently, the institutions of higher learning themselves have questioned the value of the SAT I. Many question the reliability of SAT I test results in predicting college grades. Others are concerned that our school systems, students, and parents are focusing too much time on test preparation rather than on expanding intellectual skills and knowledge.

In fact, several hundred colleges and universities no longer require the SAT I. University of California President Richard Atkinson has questioned the value of using the SAT in the admissions process, and the College Board is revising parts of the SAT I and eliminating other elements. Some of the possibilities include eliminating the analogies section in the SAT I verbal section and adding a writing sample to the exam. But no matter how the SAT I evolves, standardized testing will continue to have a significant role in the admissions process at highly selective schools, since these institutions still need a valid and reliable source that provides a baseline level for national comparison of candidates' academic credentials.

The SAT I has also become a money-making machine and part of the high school curriculum. High schools offer tutoring and test preparation classes, and third party vendors like Kaplan and the Princeton Review have lucrative businesses predicated on helping students prepare for SAT and other exams.

Longtime researcher Dean K. Whitla, who also had strong ties to the College Board, has been looking at the significance of coaching on SAT test performance for years. In one of his studies, Whitla found that Harvard students who had been coached between the first and second SAT I, when compared to Harvard students who did not receive coaching between tests, attained on average an increase of only 11 points in the verbal score and 16 points in the math score.[7] In other words, a 10 to 20 point jump per section does not constitute a significant increase. I've found, instead, that students with good study habits generally perform better the second time they take an exam, because they've familiarized themselves with the test or do a better job preparing for it.

Knowing that bright students typically score better the second time through an exam, should you spend your dollars on coaching or test prep courses? If you're the type of person who won't make the time to take practice tests or to study and prepare on your own, then registering for a course can't hurt if you have the money to spend. If financial circumstances make this difficult, however, you could work with a teacher or study the question types on your own.

Despite the hype that says preparation courses teach the secrets of the tests and the games behind them, the true value of a test course is that they are forums of learning. One studies the questions, practices the problems, and in turn develops an enhanced vocabulary, improves reading comprehension abilities, and gains a deeper understanding of mathematical concepts. This is exactly what students do in the high school classroom, so taking a test prep course should not be viewed as a panacea, but rather as a paid tutoring session. Another advantage to taking a prep course is that it requires students to make a time commitment to the classes. When I considered applying to law school and business school at various points in my life, I enrolled in the appropriate LSAT and GMAT courses. I was pleased with the structure of each class because it forced me to make a concerted effort to study and practice for the exams. Otherwise, given my family commitments and work schedule, I might not have found the necessary two to four hours a week to prepare for each practice exam.

> **TIP:** *Never take the SAT I more than three times. Scores are unlikely to improve significantly after two attempts, and since admissions offices receive all test scores, they could view students with more than three SAT scores negatively, wondering perhaps whether applicants are too test-focused.*

The Importance of AP and IB Programs

Both the Advanced Placement and the International Baccalaureate programs offer excellent preparation for university study. At the highly selective schools, these courses and scores are looked at carefully. The exams are designed based on a curriculum that aspires to the level of university work, and the results are among the best indicators of future academic performance. The growth of AP programs to expedite and reduce university graduation requirements, however, is disturbing to some.

The AP program is the College Board's largest revenue producer, and one of the criticisms of the program and its rapid growth is that the board is more interested in generating revenue than in the academic development of secondary school students. Some universities are concerned about the marketing of Advanced Placement as a way for high school students to earn college credit before they step foot in the university. Replacing college study is certainly not the goal of institutions of higher education. In fact, Ivy League administrators and faculty are beginning to limit the amount of credit an incoming student can receive for advanced study in high school.

On the other hand, universities find that AP programs are excellent preparatory vehicles for a university education. The rigorous academic curriculum and results of AP exams are also valuable and are among the most important assessment tools for admissions offices at highly selective universities.

With many high schools offering juniors, and sometimes sophomores, AP courses, admissions offices have an opportunity to review the results during the admission cycles. If you're taking an AP exam as a sophomore or a junior, remember that the results do matter. Although a score of 3 is passing for the AP, many of the most selective colleges only give college credit for scores of 4 or 5. From an admissions evaluation perspective, a score of 3 indicates an average performance in and knowledge of the subject matter.

Another point to consider: Admissions officers assume that students who are enrolled in AP level designated courses in high school will actually take the AP exam in May. If you're taking AP U.S. History as a junior and you do not submit the AP results, admissions officers may assume that you did not perform well on the test. Therefore, it's important to remember that when one chooses to enroll in an AP/IB class in secondary school, the commitment includes taking it to the very end, which means taking the tests in May.

The International Baccalaureate organization and course selection features six areas of study that demonstrate international standards while allowing students to select a more individualized program of study based upon the six core areas. University admissions committees prefer scores of 6 and 7 in Higher Level courses to results of 5 or lower or Subsidiary Level work.

At Harvard we found the IB diploma program a fairly accurate predictor of results during a student's first year of university study. As a result, our office gave credence to students who were preparing for the full diploma, had received several 6 and 7 scores in year one of the program, and had a cumulative prediction of 40 or higher on the results of six courses, with the points added for the extended essay. A number of us also appreciated the fact the program began in the junior year and emphasized a two-year curriculum.

TIP: *AP and IB tests are more highly regarded by admissions officers. Be sure to take the test results seriously and prepare for the exams.*

Taking an AP course will always benefit you in the admissions process, but there are several that are neither recognized as rigorous nor designed as programs that could be taken in lieu of college coursework. For example, we did not consider Psychology, Studio Art, and Geography as significant as other AP courses, especially since no credit was given for these tests in the Advanced Standing Program. Vertical disciplines like Chemistry, BC Calculus, and European History provide a more parallel curriculum to courses offered at Harvard, and so, among the AP courses, we gave them more credence when they were evaluated. When it comes time to decide which AP or IB courses to take, you'll still need to match your interests and plans to the courses offered at your school. You do not need to take every AP class or exam that is offered to impress an admissions office.

Co-Curricular Programs and Awards

In addition to distinguishing yourself in the classroom and through standardized testing, there are a number of summer programs, competitions, and awards that are strong indicators of intellectual and academic promise. Some of these outstanding programs have become reliable feeder systems for highly selective schools. They include competitions in math and science, as well as a handful of humanities awards.

Schools like MIT, Cal Tech, Stanford, the Ivy schools, and others aggressively recruit and compete for students who win national academic awards. The programs and competitions noted below are not an all-inclusive listing. No doubt I've overlooked some excellent programs. The academic and competitive scholarship programs I have presented regularly produce academicians and researchers in the top 1 percent of their field. Other competitive programs that consistently churn out top talent but may not provide the necessary detailed evidence of truly exceptional academic promise on their own are also listed. These programs should not be considered as the only paths for determining special academic talents, but they have historically enrolled a high caliber of student. Included in the program descriptions are links on the Web where you can find more information.

Nationally Recognized Academic Programs and Scholarship Competitions

Math and Science Olympiad Programs (U.S. and International Teams). Based upon nationally administered exams, students are selected to attend the U.S. Olympiad Camps, where a handful of students (four to six) are chosen annually to represent the United States at the respective International Olympiad competition. Attending the camp is a prestigious honor in itself, and those who attend international competitions are generally coveted by faculty within these academic departments. Some of the top international mathematicians and scientists are initially discovered and recruited to study in the United States. In all of these cases, students can speak with teachers or counselors in the appropriate subject areas on how to register to sit for any of these national exams.

U.S. and International Math Olympiad Programs. Based upon national AMC and AIME test scores, approximately 250 students are invited to take the U.S. Math Olympiad exam. From this group, 12 students attend an intensive USMO camp where 6 students will be chosen to represent the United States at the International Math Olympiad competition. Visit the American Math Associations Web site at www.unl.edu/amc/index.html for more information.

U.S. and International Chemistry Olympiad Programs. Sponsored by the American Chemical Society, 20 students are invited to attend the U.S. Chemistry Olympiad camp, where 4 are chosen to compete at the International Chemistry Olympiad. For more information, visit the students and teachers section of the Web site: www.chemistry.org.

U.S. and International Physics Olympiad Programs. Twenty-four students are invited to attend the U.S. Physics Olympiad camp and five are selected to attend the International Physics Olympiad. Visit the U.S. Physics Olympiad Team Web site: www.aapt.org/.

Research Science Institute (RSI). Sponsored by the Center for Education Excellence, RSI is probably accepted as the top summer research program in the country, and possibly the world. Each summer, 50 U.S. and 25 international high school students are selected to attend this program at the Massachusetts Institute of Technology. Often, students' summer projects turn into award-winning papers in other national competitions. Web site: www.cee.org/home/index.shtml.

Intel Science Talent Search. Formerly the Westinghouse Science Talent Search, the Intel Talent Search receives a tremendous amount of publicity and awards the first-place winner a hefty $100,000 scholarship. Students who reach the final 40 are given extremely careful consideration, and students who finish in the top 10 are almost assured a spot at one of the top schools in the country. Web site: www.intel.com/education/sts/index.htm.

Siemens Westinghouse Science and Technology Competition. Similar to the Intel competition, the Siemens Westinghouse competition (www.siemens-foundation.org) awards scholarships of $100,000 to individual and team winners in their respective categories. Top 10 finalists who apply are looked at closely. For both competitions and other research projects, admissions departments may send an applicant's research to the appropriate faculty members or departments for review when the academic distinction of the work needs further examination. The department member who conducts this review will very likely end up teaching the student at some point.

MIT MITE²S. *MITE* stands for MIT's Minority Introduction to Engineering, Entrepreneurship, and Science program. MITE²S does a great job of introducing underrepresented minority students to engineering and science at the university level. Web site: web.mit.edu/MITES.

Competitive Scholarship and Academic Programs

Competitive scholarship programs take academic achievement into account as one factor. Their selection process also considers leadership, extracurricular accomplishment, and personal character through a rigorous interviewing, screening, and assessment process. These kinds of competitive selection processes, similar to academic competitions and awards, act as filters for admissions officers to validate candidates who have been similarly identified by other organizations for talent and promise. There are many programs and regional scholarship programs. I've listed below a few of the top scholarship programs particularly noted for producing winners who year after year are among the strongest candidates for admissions to highly selective institutions.

Bronfman Youth Fellowships in Israel. The Bronfman Fellows are annually selected on the basis of character, intellectual interests, special talents and leadership qualities to participate in a five-week program in Israel. Web site: www.bronfman.org.

John Motley Morehead Scholarship Foundation. This is a full merit scholarship to the University of North Carolina at Chapel Hill that provides student-leaders summer internship experience, international travel, and study through the university. Web site:www.moreheadfoundation.org/award/.

Jefferson Scholarship Foundation. This scholarship is similar in scope to a Morehead Scholarship, but for students attending the University of Virginia. Web site: www.jeffersonscholars.org/default.asp.

Coca-Cola Scholarship Program National Award Winners. The Coca-Cola Company provides various scholarships and other programs to financially support leaders in their educational pursuits. Web site: www.cocacola.com.

Telluride Association Summer Experience. TASP has offered high-achieving students the opportunity to study topics in the humanities, social sciences, and public policy on college campuses at no expense to the student. Cornell University is one of the primary campuses involved in the program. Web site: telluride.cornell.edu.

Concord Review. The *Concord Review* is a quarterly journal focused on the publication of academic history essays and papers written by secondary school students. The high standards for publication not only identify outstanding scholarly work, but the *Review*'s rigid requirements for original academic submission also ensure the integrity of the work and organization. Web site: www.tcr.org/.

NCTE Achievement Awards in Writing. Each year, juniors are nominated by their school to participate in the National Council of Teachers of English writing competition, which evaluates and recognizes students who have shown excellence in writing. While the NCTE does select many winners, this award is a nice flag to admissions officers that the candidate has been nominated by the English Department and recognized by a national organization for one's writing abilities. Web site: www.ncte.org/grants/achieve.shtml.

Summer Math Programs. Here are a number of math programs that have produced excellent applicants to highly selective schools:

The Ross Program at Ohio State: www.math.ohio-state.edu/ross/

Stanford University Math Camp: cartan.stanford.edu/sumac/

Hampshire College Summer Studies in Math: www.hcssim.org/

To view a full listing of summer math programs for high school students visit the American Mathematical Society Web site (www.ams.org) and their summer camps page at www.ams.org/careers-edu/mathcamps.html.

National Merit and National Achievement Scholarship Programs. Based upon PSAT/NMSQT scores, National Merit Finalist (NMF) and National Achievement Scholars (NASP) are excellent starting points for admissions offices to begin the identification of top students.

Junior Classical League. Combined with summa cum laude scores on the National Latin Exam, national involvement with JCL, and a delineated interest in studying the Classics, can be a value-added academic activity.

Summer School Programs

Attending a summer school program, whether it be a "Governor's School" or a university summer program for secondary school students, can be a terrific experience. A few words of caution should be mentioned, however, before you enroll in next summer's "Prestigious University of *XX* Summer Program."

If you choose to attend a summer program, understand that grades matter. Getting a C in a class will not help you in the selective school admissions process. Also note that most of the secondary school programs generically offered by universities cost money, and admissions offices understand that there are financial limitations on many outstanding students who just can't afford to attend a summer program.

Attending a highly selective school's summer program will give you a feel for your fit at the school and should be helpful in preparing you for future academic study. But ask yourself: Could you spend your summer making an impact in areas that will resonate more effectively with an admissions officer? Could those six weeks have been dedicated to developing a new extracurricular talent, improving leadership skills, or making a difference within a community? Summer school can be a great experience—as far as admissions reps are concerned, it's certainly better than sitting on the beach—but attending summer school is not a necessity.

Academic Profile of Students Admitted to Highly Selective Colleges

The key factors that constitute an applicant's academic profile are summarized below, in the overview of academic credentials of candidates admitted to highly selective colleges and universities. Following that list, you'll see three individual academic tiers that admissions offices tend to use when categorizing admitted students. This type of profiling is a meaningful way to begin looking at admissions criteria from an admissions officer's perspective.

Overview of Academic Credentials

- At most highly selective schools, anywhere from 80 to 95 percent of the admitted students ranked in the top 10 percent of their high school class. Of these students, anywhere from 10 to 30 percent or more were class valedictorians.

- Nearly all of these students were enrolled in what college counselors would consider the most rigorous academic curriculum their high school had to offer. Only a small percentage of admitted students would have been enrolled in a very demanding, second-tier curriculum, or lower.

- Most students admitted to highly selective schools will have taken at least one AP or IB exam prior to beginning college. Well over half will have taken at least one AP or IB exam prior to the beginning of their senior year in high school.

- More than three-fourths of students admitted to highly selective schools will have SAT I scores above 1250. Approximately 25 percent will have SAT I scores above 1450, and at approximately 15 of the most highly selective institutions, 25 percent of the admitted students will score above 1500.

The Academic Tiers

Top 5 Percent. This tier includes those who are national academic scholars, heavily recruited, and those students whose clear-cut admission is based on academic credentials alone.

- These students represent the top 5 percent of the admitted student body at highly selective colleges.

- Almost all of these candidates are in the top 1 to 2 percent of their high school graduating class and are enrolled in the most demanding curriculum offered at their school.

- Most of these students have SAT I and SAT II test scores in the 770 range or higher across the board, including several 800s.

- These students have taken multiple AP and/or IB exams and have scored the highest results possible (AP scores of 5 and IB scores of 7).

- Many of these students have enrolled, or were enrolled at the time of admission, in university coursework in their particular fields of interest during the summer or during the term year.

- These students have been recognized nationally by winning academic national and international competitions (such as those

49

listed in the co-curricular programs), by scoring in the top 1 percent in national testing, by participating in prestigious programs mentored by university professors, or by other means that are recognized by admissions offices and university faculty alike.

- Many of these candidates' applications were reviewed by professors in the student's field of interest and received strong endorsements.

- Often, the faculty members of the institutions that are competing for the candidate help to recruit these students.

The 1400 Club. These students are academic scholars and strong contenders for admission based on their academic credentials.

- Those admitted from this group represent the largest percentage of the student body at the most selective institutions, comprising 65 to 75 percent of the admitted population. These students are strong academic talents across the board, close to national scholars, though they may not have been the recipients of national academic acclaim. Their admission will not be based on academic performance alone.

- These students rank in the top 5 to 10 percent of the high school graduating class, and many of these admitted students were valedictorians or salutatorians.

- Their SAT I scores are typically in the 1400 to 1550 range and higher. Most of these students' SAT II scores are in the mid-700 or higher range.

- They are enrolled in the most demanding curriculum in high school, and nearly all of them have taken an AP/IB exam prior to senior year of high school and scored well on these exams, with APs of 4 and 5 and IB scores of 6 and 7.

- The main difference between these candidates and those recognized as national scholars who are viewed as "clear admits" is that these candidates most likely have not won the type of national recognition through testing, competition, or other programs to warrant placement into the most elite academic category.

- Some of these students may have had their applications and papers reviewed by faculty and they might not have been regarded as among the top students in their academic interest. More bluntly, the accomplishments of the candidate may not have particularly impressed the faculty member(s).

- These candidates had strong letters of recommendation from academic teachers to help elevate their candidacy above those with similar academic credentials who were not offered admission.

- Academically, these candidates are as strong as any student in any applicant pool; however, their application needed factors outside of the academic realm to seal their acceptance letter, such as distinguished extracurricular achievements and solid personal qualities.

Better than the National Average. These students are solid but not distinguished academic candidates.

- Students admitted from this group comprise 25 to 35 percent of the class at highly selective schools.

- Most of these students are ranked in the top 10 percent of the high school graduating class, though many may have only been in the top 20 percent.

- The SAT I scores for most of these candidates range from 1200 to 1350, though a percentage of these students may have scores below 1200. Upward of 10 percent of all admitted applicants at highly selective schools may have test scores below 1200.

- SAT I and SAT II scores will have a much greater variance among this group, since many of these admitted students will have shown stronger aptitude within specific academic disciplines.

- Nearly all of the students admitted from this tier will have completed an AP or IB level course upon graduating from high school, though a small percentage will not have taken the exam. Test scores will cover a broad range, with typical AP results of 3, 4, and 5, and IB results of 5, 6, and 7.

- Most of these students are enrolled in the most demanding programs in their school. Some of them are in school systems that provide as challenging a college preparatory program as other high schools. Those who are in a second-tier academic program are typically at a school that has a wealth of academic offerings and thus, a second-tier program is still a solid preparatory environment.

- Many students in this category have had fewer academic opportunities for advancement: limited schools systems, weaker academic curriculum, and lack of opportunity for concurrent summer or university level study during high school.

- This group of students is assessed as being capable of handling the academic rigors of a highly selective institution, but the leading factor for admission is not an academic tip. Instead, all of these candidates had other distinguishing factors that led the admissions office to admit them.

Endnotes

1. *Early Action* is one form of early admissions available for candidates interested in submitting an application to a school in the late fall to receive an admissions decision prior to the traditional April mailing date. Early admissions is discussed in more detail in Chapter 6.

2. Brent Bridgeman, Laura Mcamley-Jenkins, and Nancy Ervin, "Prediction of Freshman Grade Point Average from the Revised and Recentered SAT I Reasoning Test," in *College Entrance Examination Board, 2000,* Table 4, p. 5, www.collegeboard.com/repository/rr0001_3917.pdf (June 2002).

3. Thomas J. Stanley, *The Mind of a Millionaire* (Kansas City, Missouri: Andrews McMeel Publishing, 2000), p. 13.

4. "1998 Profile of College Board Seniors National Report," www.collegeboard.org/sat/cbsenior/yr1998/nat/natsdm.html (April 2002).

5. Harvard College Undergraduate Office of Admissions, class of 2003 SAT applicant data report.

6. "The College Board Announces a New SAT," www.college board.com/press/article/0,3183,11147.html (June 27, 2002).

7. Dean K. Whitla, "Coaching: Does It Pay? Not for Harvard Students," *The College Board Review*, No. 148, Summer 1988.

EXTRACURRICULAR ACTIVITIES

Making a Difference on and off Campus

Knowing that the overwhelming majority of candidates who apply to selective colleges and universities can handle the academic workload, what additional factors most influence the decisions that admissions offices make when choosing between them?

While there are many tangible and intangible dynamics that shape the strengths and merits of an applicant's case, the most significant nonacademic factor in the admissions process for nearly all of the top institutions is the extracurricular experiences of candidates. Visit any of the Ivy League or other highly selective campuses and you'll see evidence of a range of community activities, social events, and political involvement, all of which make the experience of living in a university setting unique. Admissions officers, recognizing the importance of extracurricular activities, help shape campus life by seeking candidates who bring passion and experience—a résumé, if you will—for the many activities and organizations that make an undergraduate "education" so stimulating away from the classroom.

Why are extracurricular activities, often referred to as ECs or ECAs in admissions offices, so important in the decision-making process?

Evaluating your ECAs serve a twofold purpose. First, they provide a competitive assessment tool for choosing from among the 80 to 85 percent of applicants who are academically qualified. And second, ECAs are a way to find leaders and top talent in nonacademic areas who will not only contribute to campus and community life, but also show potential to serve as leaders in society after they graduate.

From a broad perspective, admissions offices look to evaluate three components of a student's extracurricular activities:

- The breadth and depth of an applicant's activities
- The candidate's EC activities and accomplishments compared to others, from a "coast-to-coast" perspective
- The extent to which these activities indicate how a candidate might make an impact on a college campus

Breadth and depth. The level of involvement of students in extracurricular activities is assessed by considering how they balance involvement in a number of activities while also being able to excel in one or two of them. This is an important method for examining how multidimensional a candidate is, compared to those who develop a "specialized" skill set in one particular area.

Comparison. Applicants with similar ECA experiences are compared to one another to gauge how strong their accomplishments are relative to peers participating in similar activities. Candidates' activities are also measured against those with talents in other ECAs in order to assess the top talents from various areas and compare the breadth of involvement for those candidates. Admissions offices also attempt to measure how candidates have taken advantage of the resources available to them. Some students may face obstacles because of family, school, community, or financial resources, while others may have engaged in fewer extracurricular activities because the resources weren't available. Considering how applicants take advantage of the available opportunities certainly says something about them.

Campus impact. Admissions officers want to know how an applicant's activities and experiences might presage their involvement on campus, or in some cases, how these talents might be developed after college. Local high school, regional, or national involvement can often foretell the contributions a candidate might make on campus. Assessing whether those talents might blossom beyond college is less certain, but there is value in considering what admissions officers term a "futures test"—a standard by which they discuss what a candidate might do in the future based upon what is compelling in the application. Although admissions officers are not experts at looking into a crystal ball and making bold predictions, they do possess the ability to detect special talents that might unfurl during and after college. We'll talk about the relationship of a student's interests and its relation with the "futures test" when we examine how it can sway an admissions case.

Taking these three components into account enable admissions staffs to look beyond the academic record and to differentiate between candidates who have not placed in the top 1 to 5 percent of the admissions pool after review by departmental faculty. Remember, we've already addressed just how few students are admitted annually solely for academic prowess. Colleges and universities are dynamic places, with more to offer than a lecture hall or a research facility, and administrators want to continue to foster involvement in programs that help to make the undergraduate experience exciting and rewarding. Finally, the top institutions are seeking to admit, train, and educate leaders for the twenty-first century. Political, musical, athletic, or business leaders can be as accomplished outside of the high school/college classroom as in them, or even more so.

Let's take a closer look at how admissions offices evaluate specific high school programs and activities, and highlight how the plethora of student groups and programs that exist on college campuses across the country can provide a springboard for growth and development in the extracurricular world.

The Extracurricular Milieu

Look at admissions publications, application guides, or other marketing materials for any of the top institutions and you'll find strong references to the variety and world-class caliber of the extracurricular activities on their respective campuses. Most of a college's numerous extracurricular offerings can be categorized into academic/educational, cultural/ethnic, performing arts, athletics, service, politics/government, religious, publications/media, and clubs/hobbies.

The range of opportunities available to students nowadays is astonishing. For example, there are at least 17 recognized a cappella, choral, and other vocal groups at the University of Pennsylvania. There are more than 20 different publications at Columbia, 41 varsity-level sports programs at Harvard, and over 70 different community service groups at Yale. If there is a way to make an impact on college life, students find a way to do it. In fact, while living in the dorms for three years as an academic adviser, I discovered that many of the students I advised identified themselves more by their nonacademic activities than their academic interests.

The huge range of interests of my students was simply energizing. Of the activities in which the 26 to 28 students I advised annually participated, vocal groups, athletics, musical organizations, and community service were by far the four areas of greatest interest. But there were several students each year who made meaningful contributions to other activities or organizations.

Extend this type of energy to a campus with 200 to 300 or more organizations, and their attendant groups and programs, and it's easy to understand how students provide the critical lifeblood to a college. They can create, enhance, or change the personality of an institution. In addition, a student population active in an array of extracurricular programs will make a significant impact on the community. A politically active campus, a service-oriented student body, or a musically diverse campus is crucial in building a vibrant community for students.

In recent years institutions have made serious improvements in the quality of nonacademic programs, with improvements to facilities such as music halls, student unions, and athletic facilities. Capital improvements on Ivy League campuses since 1998 include: Princeton's stadium, a $48 million football and indoor track facility; Yale's Gilmore Music Library, an $11 million project; and Cornell's recently dedicated Schwartz Center for Performing Arts, a $25 million project. And leading universities continue to focus alumni relations and capital campaigns around improving university facilities, which become key recruiting elements in attracting top students and faculty.

If you're fortunate enough to live near a residential college, you know that on any given night there are multiple entertainment options revolving around nonacademic student activities. Whether it's a poetry reading, a theatrical event, or a concert, there's never a problem finding something to do. The many nonacademic organizations also form the student infrastructure of the university's school newspaper and other publications, peer counseling, student government, and community service and advocacy groups. In some cases, students extend their involvement beyond the school walls and into the larger town or city community.

Clearly there are many ways to contribute to the college environment. Recognizing the importance of student activities, admissions offices attempt to support a vibrant campus by admitting students who will become involved with existing opportunities or seek to spark new programs and make a difference.

Depth versus Breadth of Extracurricular Commitments

In determining the weight that extracurricular activities should carry in an application, admissions offices look for a balance between the breadth and depth of a candidate's involvement. Ask any admissions representative what is more important, having a wide range of activities or having one or two strong areas of interest, and you'll be told they're looking for both. But while application readers appreciate the value of being involved in a variety of activities outside the classroom, they expect that some of the most competitive candidates will be students who show a special depth of talent, sense of leadership, or serious commitment to an activity.

Measuring the depth of individual programs can be a challenge. With an extensive variety of school, community, and personal activities for a student to pursue, and with all the regional, state, and national options, it can be difficult to state that one activity or program is more important than another. Assessing ECAs is a continuous process of examining what an applicant has done in the past, what he or she is doing now, and what he or she will be doing in the future, all in the context of the level of accomplishment and involvement. Looking at the extracurricular activities sheet or résumé is an inexact science at best; but admissions officers are trained to evaluate ECAs on their own merits, in the larger context of how they round out the full application, and in the still larger context of how one applicant's ECAs compare to those of others in the entire applicant pool.

Addressing the breadth and depth of one's involvement is an interesting balancing act. I've read lots of applications from students who decided to be part of every group and garner as many trophy leadership positions as possible. However, once I delved into the activities and the substance of those leadership roles, the degree to which these positions made an impact on the surrounding community, or didn't, became evident. A common case was that of the junior or senior who had not been particularly active outside the classroom for two-plus years of high school suddenly deciding to join as many clubs and organizations as possible in order to build a résumé that would show a breadth of involvement. All things considered, I generally preferred reading about more substantive activities in fewer areas of interest than seeing a list of activities that screamed "Jack of all trades, master of none!"

Then there are those students who make the college visits in the summer, prior to their senior year of high school, or who sit down with a college counselor during the spring of their junior or fall of their senior year and realize that their record does not show a strong or diverse set of extracurricular activities. While joining clubs and organizations late is better than not at all, the rationale for these efforts is fairly transparent to admissions officers and will not endear you to them. On the other hand, there's always an opportunity to make a difference, even later in high school.

> **TIP:** *Don't wait until senior year to join clubs and organizations in order to build a "laundry list" of activities. If you haven't been involved in many extracurricular activities prior to senior year, you should find one or two that excite you and make a difference in them.*

For those who jump into activities or find themselves in leadership positions, it's essential to make a meaningful contribution. When it comes time to make choices among candidates, admissions officers look at the Letters of Recommendation for insight, since advisers, coaches, and adult supervisors are among the best resources for providing more details on a student's level of commitment to an activity. Student government officer positions, for example, are notorious for being a popularity contest where the title is more of a badge than a true leadership position. A good admissions officer can easily recognize the speciousness of the position when little is written by the student or by the counselor in the application. A lack of detail or a description of the responsibilities leads admissions officers to question whether a student has a true interest in that activity. Students can highlight their leadership roles and responsibilities either by providing a short description of the organization along with examples of the impact they made, or by having a Letter of Recommendation from someone who knows the candidate's contribution well added to the application file.

TIP: *If you have an extracurricular adviser, coach, or mentor who can write an in-depth letter of recommendation about your commitment, leadership, or contributions, ask them to write on your behalf. You should not have more than one or two supplementary letters added to your application, unless specifically asked to do so by an admissions officer.*

Avoiding Tunnel Vision

On the other side of the issue are those students who are so engaged in one or two activities that they seem to have tunnel vision, or appear one-dimensional. An application can overcome this stereotype if the student is exceptional at that activity or if members of an admissions committee can see those skills as transferable to somewhere on campus. Even in these cases, however, a student who participates in and excels in only one or two activities will need to be recognized nationally, or at the very least regionally, for that activity to be a key factor in gaining admission. Nearly all students who have a single special talent still have a few other avenues of interest to complement their main talents. Even the best musical aficionados, the most acclaimed thespians, and the most heavily recruited athletes need to offer solid grades, test scores, and personal qualities to make it through the process.

Admissions officers will evaluate the depth and achievements in your extracurricular activities. Through years of experience, they can recognize activities that show a real return on the time and energy invested by a candidate. Most admissions offices also have staff members who have knowledge and interests in a broad range of activities, so you need not be concerned that the EC commitments you have undertaken will not be acknowledged. At Harvard, for instance, where I was not particularly well-versed in evaluating the various media used in studio art, I was able to work with a Fine Arts major and several others with a penchant for the visual arts, and they kept a watchful eye for candidates with special talents in painting, sculpting, and other art forms.

Understanding the school, the community, and the region of the country also helps admissions officers understand the contributions students have made to their communities. There may be opportunities to make an impact within the school based on the school's size or the financial resources available for funding nonacademic programs. There may be a very different set of choices available to a student living in a rural setting than in an urban environment. Understanding the local flavor—what it means to be the seminary president in a Utah school, to be the head of a local search and rescue organization in the Arizona desert, or to be the first chair clarinet in the all-state band of North Carolina—also helps admissions staffs evaluate students from coast-to-coast on a more level playing field. As a student, evaluate your own involvement in ECAs by considering how the activities in which you've participated have made an impact on your community and how they stand out or are unique.

The real key for evaluating the true strength of ECAs in an application is to look for and examine the individual's passion for the activities. An admissions officer can see how many hours per week a candidate puts into an activity and can read the list of awards and titles received, but nothing spotlights a student more clearly than a genuine zeal and energy for an activity. This passion and depth are typically evident in a student's essays or short answers, an interview, and letters of recommendation. When that dedication for an activity pervades an application, an admissions staff can envision how it can add more life to a college campus.

It follows that if a student really loves something, she shouldn't be shy about discussing it. Readers want to learn more about her passions and what those passions say about her. Having a résumé that lists the range of awards of the National Forensics League (NFL), which is a prestigious debating organization, along with essays and letters that validate that the student is not only the seventh place finisher in the NFL Extemp category at the nationals but has shown positive leadership skills, will impress any admissions committee. It might be nice if the student continues to debate in college, but positive feedback from teachers and coaches, or an essay that addresses the impact of the experiences, will nevertheless suggest that she would fit well on campus, whether she continues to debate in college or not. This kind of combination will carry far more weight than being a national champion—rather than the seventh place finisher—who does not display complementary leadership or personal skills.

Another thing an admissions office notices—only in this case negatively—is the candidate who blindly searches for the golden chalice. Many students have attained titles and other awards of significance because it's what their parents and others expect of them. As admissions candidates, some of these students are highly competitive and off-putting, while others are simply fulfilling the parent-child social contract of twenty-first-century suburban America, where high school students are reacting to the demands of parents who push them to succeed in order to prepare for college admittance. In both cases, the laundry list of awards and leadership positions come across as programmed and sterile, especially when compared to the involvement of those students who are able to demonstrate a true passion.

Every year, students are disillusioned at the end of the admissions process when they're not admitted to any of the top-tiered schools, despite having done everything they were supposed to have done in and out of the classroom. For many, it truly may have been the luck of the draw and the fact that there just are not enough available spaces for all of the great candidates. A good number of these students were likely viewed as "standard strong" applicants. Some of the locally strong ECs that stand out within the school can be viewed as "standard strong" when compared nationally to others with similar local experiences. Officers of student government, the National Honor Society, debate captains, and captains of a sports team begin to blend in with the thousands of other candidates with similar credentials. It is important, therefore, to have additional strengths to beef up a locally strong portfolio of extracurricular activities. Because it is very hard to stand out academically, given the amazing academic firepower of applicants that we discussed earlier, it's the ECAs and personal qualities that separate the wheat from the chaff.

TIP: *A genuine time commitment and examples of success and leadership in the application can help your activities rise above those of the "standard strong" applicants.*

Ultimately, a student needs to find his niche and make a difference or contribution in the best way he knows how. Considering the kinds of activities that impress admissions readers, extracurricular activities can be broadly defined as traditional and nontraditional. The nontraditional activities are pursuits that tend to be more individual, are not always highly organized on a national level, and do not receive a tremendous amount of funding at the university level. Admissions committees do not look upon nontraditional or unique ECAs as less important, but they're much more difficult to describe or place into one defined category.

For the extracurricular activities not discussed in this section, or for pursuits that are more personal in nature, it's important to note that the significance an activity has as it pertains to the admissions process is related to the importance and impact of that activity on an individual and those around him or her. While I won't be able to review all of the amazing organizations and ECAs that have for years been seen as strong indicators of special talents and leadership, let's look at some of the areas that have resonated positively within admissions offices.

Student Government and the Politicians of Tomorrow

At all of the leading universities, politics and government play an important role in shaping the undergraduate students' lives. Likewise, admissions officers are searching for candidates who show qualities that will translate well in on-campus political organizations and potentially beyond a student's college days. In addition, student government is an important and high profile activity within the high schools across the United States. The depth of leadership derived from this genre of activity comes from the commitment of the school to these programs.

High schools that give an active voice to SGA officers not only create opportunity for young adults to emerge as leaders within the community, but also provide a vehicle for students to stand apart from their peers across the country who are also presidents and vice presidents of the student body. Within larger schools, the president of the student body is seen as the leading student government position, but it might be surprising to some to hear that class presidents were often viewed as more prestigious and impressive than other associated student body positions. Generally, associated student body officers are considered more significant than class officers, but being a president at any level has extra cachet with admissions readers.

In some states, student government positions bring individual high school officers together from throughout the state. These positions are not necessarily viewed with greater acclaim by admissions offices since they don't all mean the same thing. For example, in some states the time commitment is not much more than the organization of a weekend event to discuss issues. As the area admissions officer for Indiana and Illinois, I had the opportunity to review applications from students who were officers in statewide student government organizations. Although I try to refrain from making sweeping judgments, from everything I read, it seemed that the state of Illinois student government officers were more involved and had more responsibility than their Indiana counterparts.

On a local level, school systems that actually give their student government officers the opportunity to affect change and advocate on behalf of the student body put their students at an advantage when applying to highly selective schools. For example, the case for admission might be bolstered for a student body president or vice president who leads a task force to implement changes to a school's daily class schedule or creates a comprehensive tutoring program that is successfully implemented and services hundreds of at-risk students a semester. One way in which school systems have sought to engage their top leaders is through the creation of nonvoting student members of the school committee. This type of "student representative/adviser" position can be very valuable, but it is also heavily dependent on the initiative of the student.

I sat in on several school committee meetings in Quincy, Massachusetts, where only one of the three to four students who represented the two high schools made any type of contribution to the school committee meetings. While the honor of being selected to represent the student voice in the committee meeting is nice, it would be more impressive if the school superintendent or the members of the committee wrote a meaningful, supportive letter that would highlight students on the committee.

There are a number of regional and national programs that look terrific on any student's résumé, and it's possible to make an impact in town and state politics as an individual. But there are three programs in particular that receive high-level praise and acceptance in admissions circles. The most renowned is the American Legion and American Legion Auxiliary's sponsorship of Boys and Girls State and Boys and Girls Nation, which engage youth in politics. Former President Bill Clinton, a Boys State and Nation alumnus, has given this program a tremendous amount of awareness.

Boys and Girls State programs are conducted on the state level and designed to help develop leadership skills and provide instruction on the principles of state and national government. On the state level, typically, one or two students are selected from each high school to attend the weeklong state conference. At the end of the week, students are elected to political offices, the most prestigious being governor, lieutenant governor, and attorney general. From these events, each state program selects two students to attend Boys Nation and Girls Nation in Washington, D.C.

Students who receive the honor of attending the Nation programs are at a significant advantage in the admissions process. They have gone through competitive selection on a number of levels. They were recommended on the local level and succeeded in winning over their peers at the state level. Usually these students have extraordinary personal skills, and their recommendations and interviews reveal these traits. Unless the academics are less competitive, Boys and Girls Nation candidates hold up well in the national comparison to other applicants.

Another program that is very rigorous is the U.S. Senate Page School. Juniors in high school can apply for this program, and those selected as Senate pages work full days for their United States senator while also maintaining a demanding school schedule. Pages attend school from 6 a.m. until the Senate session begins, and then often work until 6 p.m. or later. This program has always been held in high esteem, but the grueling job of a page can take a toll on a student's academic performance. When a student can continue to maintain strong academics, then she or he is assumed to possess the maturity and the time management skills needed to be ready for the demands of college.

The third program that impresses admissions committees is the Senate Youth Scholarship Program, in which scholarships are given to state residents who are members of their school's student government. While it does not require attendance at a weeklong conference or a yearlong commitment, the selection process helps identify students who have made a difference in their school or regional civic organizations.

In some instances there are intersections that highlight a candidate's commitment and interest in political and civic action. One applicant I came across, from a public high school in Torrance, California, exemplified how an in-depth passion for politics and government positively impacts an application. Within the school, she held the less prominent elected position as student body treasurer. She was also engaged in the City Youth Forum outside of school, and her leadership qualities were evident and recognized, as teachers selected her to attend Girls State. While the applicant was engaged in other activities, this was clearly her distinguishing extracurricular excellence.

For others, student government and politics become a valuable compliment to a broader skill set. An applicant from a private school in Boston, for example, was active as class vice president, but at the same time, this candidate's passion for the arts and sailing (team cocaptain) took center stage over student government. Putting the pieces together, the consistent level of accomplishment and leadership within the school had as significant an impact on the admissions decision as the candidate whose activities evolved at the regional and state level.

The Great Debate

Debate is considered a valuable extracurricular activity because those who excel regionally and nationally have important speaking and presentation skills that translate well in college. Debate is also perceived as an academic activity, given its emphasis on research within the humanities, social sciences, and other liberal arts.

Some universities actively recruit and offer scholarships to national caliber debaters. The University of Michigan, USC, Emory, and Northwestern, for instance, offer scholarships to top candidates who have shown academic promise in addition to public speaking and debating talents. Without getting mired too deeply in detail, there are two main organizations and several debating events that are recognized as the most prestigious and highest in caliber. The National Forensics League (NFL) and the Catholic Forensics League (CFL) are two of them, and their Extemp, Lincoln-Douglas, and Policy Debate categories reign as leading formats in the debating world.

Lincoln-Douglas and Extemp are individual events that address several topics throughout the year, while in Policy Debate, considered by some to be the most competitive, a two-person team addresses a single national topic throughout the year. Policy Debate is heavily research oriented, so it's not surprising that many of the candidates with this background are considered excellent researchers.

The debating circuit is both regional and national, and students can rise to national status in a variety of ways. While there are many events, much like the pro golfing tour, a handful of events have risen to elite status. The NFL Tournament is considered the national championships in debate, while the Tournament of Champions, hosted by the University of Kentucky, and the CFL Tournament are other leading events in the debating world. In addition, there are a number of events hosted by high schools and universities annually that draw top talent and award winners. Events held at the Montgomery Bell Academy in Tennessee, the Greenhill School in Texas, the Glenbrook Schools in Illinois as well as Emory, Harvard, and Northwestern universities offer debaters the opportunity to shine.

Like any other skill or talent, great debaters need lots of practice and good coaching, and a number of strong summer debating programs provide novices with the opportunity to improve their skills and network with peers and mentors. Many of the top high school programs send students to these summer experiences to help them learn to master their events. Among the many offered, Dartmouth, Michigan, Kentucky, Northwestern, Iowa, and Stanford all have notable summer programs.

Strong debaters are considered very carefully among admissions officers who understand the debating hierarchy, the relative competitiveness, and the prestige of the awards received in forensics competition. Strong personal qualities and excellent communication skills are hallmarks of a stellar debater. At the same time, a small handful of debating applicants have to be cautious about the aggressive and hard-charging nature of the activity. Some students can pull too much of their debating abilities into the application with writing that portrays the tone of a policy debate research brief, and this can be a serious turnoff to readers. For these candidates, good letters of recommendation and emphasizing balance in the application will round out a top debater's achievements effectively.

Music and Visual and Performing Arts: High Profile on Campus and in Admissions

Along with athletics, music is an extracurricular activity where admissions offices can evaluate an individual's talents and place a value on it in relation to institutional needs and priorities. Highly selective institutions hold music in high regard, considering it both an academic pursuit and an extracurricular activity. NYU, Yale, and Columbia offer renowned conservatory programs in addition to their strong academic departments. Music departments at other schools offer individualized instruction and opportunities to perform on campus and within the music scene in the area.

From an admissions perspective, the greatest emphasis is typically placed on traditional instruments; that is, those used in classical, symphonic, and orchestral music. Jazz music, composition, and vocal music are also weighed heavily; but most of the nonvocalist musicians who are admitted show a strong interest and talent in orchestral music. Students interested in participating in the school band also receive consideration, but this is less evident at schools that do not have Big Ten–type marching bands.

73

One reason admissions offices can identify and admit outstanding musicians is the willingness of the music faculty at selective schools to audition leading talents or review music tapes applicants submit as supplemental materials. As schools look to develop successful music programs, many admissions offices work closely with the music departments to identify top musicians in the applicant pool. At Harvard, more music tapes are submitted to the admissions office each year than could possibly be reviewed by department faculty. The application becomes an important filtering tool, with tapes forwarded to the appropriate faculty members based on a student's résumé, experience, and letters of recommendation, in relation to his or her musical talents. In order to screen and evaluate a candidate's portfolio effectively, it's important for readers to understand the needs of the campus music programs for that particular year. Some years, the jazz band may be in particular need of a percussionist, or the orchestra may be short of French horns or bassists.

Certain instruments are perpetually in need, and this can benefit a very good musician who is committed to participating in musical activities on campus. The harp, French horn, double bass, oboe, bassoon, and certain types of percussion instruments are among those that are in constant demand at any campus looking to continue its musical excellence. Whether one plays a less prominent or a more popular instrument, there are levels of competition at colleges based upon the size of the music program and the draw in the applicant pool for particular instrument types. Piano, violin, and alto saxophone annually dominate the ranks of admissions in both number and the depth of talent, and as tapes are reviewed, the standards by which a candidate will be assessed rises according to the talent level on campus. For example, there are only so many seats available for violinists in the leading symphonies and orchestras, and there may be a limited number of faculty to work only with the top handful of violinists. While it might be hard for an admissions office to turn away a nationally recognized pianist, if there are similarly qualified pianists, those with the strongest academic credentials and most compelling personal qualities will be at a significant advantage. In assessing musical talents, candidates who have auditioned for the music department or have had a tape review will be in a better position in the context of the greater application pool, since they will have provided a basis for comparison. Of the thousands of tapes submitted to admissions, several hundred are filtered to the appropriate university departments for review. About 20 percent of the music cases reviewed will be classified as truly outstanding nationally by the faculty, as good as any performers on campus, or as one of the top players in the applicant pool. During my last year of admissions at Harvard, our office wanted to track the admissions rate of candidates evaluated by the music faculty. Of the 56 music tapes evaluated as truly outstanding, nationally competitive for the class of 2004, about 34 candidates were admitted and 5 were placed on the waiting list, an admit rate of almost 61 percent.

It should be noted that reviewing music through taped performance does have its limitations. Players of less standard instruments like the sitar, Native American flute, or the Irish fiddle will still be judged heavily on previous levels of achievements or awards, but they may not receive the benefit of a formal faculty review. In some cases, this lack of review may not be as important as the value that the student who possesses this skill will bring to campus.

Music evaluations are usually helpful, as you might have surmised. Students who are evaluated as truly outstanding or who will contribute to music life on campus will get a boost in the application process. Keep in mind that a tape of your performance will probably be the only chance the music faculty will have to review your performance. When making a tape or burning a CD, the quality of the recording is important. If a recording is distorted or difficult to hear due to static, it will be challenging for the music department to assess your technical skills accurately.

TIP: *If you're going to take the time to record a music tape or CD for review, be certain to make a high-quality copy for a clear assessment by potential listeners.*

Music ratings and evaluations allow admissions officers to not only compare a student's talent among other violists or clarinetists, but also to create a standard that permits relative comparisons to other extracurricular pursuits. A nationally rated trombonist may be compared to a national policy debate champion or to a statewide 4-H president. Using these kinds of comparative tools better equip admissions officers for the difficult choices that must be made each year.

A number of great programs are solid indicators that an applicant may be exceptional. Applicants who have attended the Interlochen or Tanglewood summer music programs are regularly rated as top musical talents. Youth symphony orchestras, such as the Chicago Youth Symphony Orchestra, have also produced nationally acclaimed talents, and the National Youth Symphony and American Youth Philharmonic are also very good proving grounds.

Awards, such as concertmaster of the largest regional and national orchestras, will also highlight top musicians among the applicant pool, and national concerto winners at the Kennedy Center or Carnegie Hall will identify national caliber musicians as well. Conservatory programs such as Case Western or the New England Conservatory, solid training programs, also help identify top candidates who ought to be reviewed by music faculty, even if they're not necessarily among the top 1 percent. And performing at a major concert hall can be a boost to an application, but sometimes this raises questions: Was the performance a solo or was the performer a participant in a larger group? Did the performer win a regional or national competition that brought the candidate to the main stage?

The formula for identifying promising candidates in the areas of jazz music and the marching band is the same. Those who have performed at local jazz festivals and on the national scene highlight their talent; the Newport, Montreal, and Montrose Jazz Festivals are among the top venues. Occasionally, highly selective schools have the opportunity to see an applicant who has participated in the Grammy High School Jazz Ensemble. These candidates are selected from across the country and come together to perform, rehearse, and create a CD around the time of the Grammy Awards. Members of the marching band are most likely identified through all-state status, but potential band members do not get the same boost in admissions that a top violinist or an alto saxophonist might get. For a marching band tuba player to get that extra push, he or she will need a solid music review.

Assessing the skill level of an applicant involved in the performing arts can be a more ambiguous process. Reviewing videotapes is an extremely cumbersome activity for admissions officers and faculty members alike. In only a handful of instances will a videotape be reviewed outside of the admissions office, and then only if the résumé of the candidate seems strong. Nonetheless, dance, theater, visual arts, and other performance areas are considered important activities on university campuses. Of course, with so many different opportunities for performance, some activities will be more in the forefront and on the minds of readers than others. Musical theater, drama, jazz dance, ballet, and ethnic dance are understood reasonably well within admissions circles. Schools with large programs or strong reputations in the arts will have no problems articulating the comparative levels of achievement in these areas for their students; while those engaged in community-oriented programs may wish to offer more details or explanation about their commitment levels.

Similar to the performing arts, much of the assessment of the visual arts will occur within the admissions office. In some cases, truly exceptional work or art media, which an admissions office may not be equipped to assess, will be brought to the attention of university members who have a greater knowledge of the form(s). For the most part, however, a candidate's portfolio or art slides will not be evaluated by trained faculty or Fine Arts majors who work in the admissions office.

That being said, visual artists have an opportunity to appeal to the senses and interests of a more or less inexperienced group of art "experts." Admittedly, I am not an expert in the visual arts, but I can give you some insight on what to avoid should you be interested in submitting supplementary artwork. First, do not submit large and thick portfolios for review unless the admissions office specifically asks you to do so. Readers simply do not have the time to review a mammoth portfolio the way it ought to be evaluated. Second, focus your selections to highlight your best work and to show your range of talent in different media, keeping in mind the amount of time it might take an admissions representative to review your portfolio. Third, if you have the resources, send slides of your work.

TIP: *When submitting any supplemental work, music or art, less is always more. It is preferred that you send just your best work, since it will stand out, than to add pieces of lesser quality that may detract from your strength(s).*

Ultimately, there's a tremendous amount of latitude given to admissions offices in assessing music, visual arts, and drama/theater activities. In many offices, assessing students' talents in these areas is one of the more inspiring and exciting aspects of the admissions job. Candidates who excel in these areas nationally are at an advantage, but there is a significant amount of regional flavor in these activities when one takes into account cultural, ethnic, and geographic influences on the arts.

Power of the Pen: Publications, Journalism, and Writing

Involvement in writing and participation in media publications have been among the more traditional activities for high school students. Serious involvement in print and other media channels is a great way to make an impact and be noticed by admission officers.

The range of possibilities and opportunities for students interested in developing their writing skills is enormous. At the high school level, the most common publication is the school newspaper, and the prestigious position on the paper is the editor in chief. Similar to the tenor of our discussions throughout this chapter, the position is only as valuable as the level of commitment shown by the applicant. How many hours per week are spent working on the publication? How often will it be published? How many contributors participate in the publication? These are the questions admissions boards seek to answer.

Copy editors and section editors are also good positions to have, along with contributing writer positions; however, admissions offices are interested in seeing the fruits of one's labor. It is more than appropriate to include several articles as supplementary material if you write for the newspaper, or to send in an edition of a recently produced paper if you have an editing position. It can also be helpful to have the faculty adviser or an editor write a note outlining your commitment to the newspaper.

Many students take their writing a step further by getting involved with the local newspaper. Writing or interning for the local paper is definitely a feather in one's cap, but again, the level of the commitment will be assessed in the application. There's also a distinction made between those who write in a weekly teen section and those few journalists or interns who have more significant responsibilities. Can the articles make it into other sections of the daily paper? A positive letter from the paper's editor or from the department can add to the depth of the application.

At some schools the yearbook is a massive undertaking, which makes the position of editor in chief an important one. Yearbook contributors typically do not receive a tremendous amount of fanfare or praise within the school, but admissions readers do not forget the key players in the yearbook, particularly at schools that have large student populations or outstanding traditions. Budding journalists may also choose to take advantage of some wonderful summer opportunities, such as the Northwestern and Ball State summer journalism schools.

Other students choose to participate as writers through literary magazines. Admissions committees identify outstanding writers through school literary magazines. What's more, next to the personal essay, a quality literary submission can be a major reason for an admissions officer to request a humanities professor to review a candidate's application and writing sample. Although the scope of literary magazines in high school mainly focus on fiction, poetry, essays, and art, some students have taken the initiative to expand their literary offerings within the school. But while a student will certainly be noticed for creating a new paper, journal, or magazine, the importance placed on any publication by an admissions office still calls upon commitment, teamwork, quality, and the frequency of that publication.

Entrepreneurship, Business Internships, and Term-Time Work

Some of the most interesting applicants in a highly selective school's pool are budding capitalists and young entrepreneurs. Some work to support themselves and their families, while others have a penchant for developing ideas. There are some incredibly creative individuals who choose to start a business and pursue a venture of interest to them, and others who choose to work interesting summer and term-time jobs.

I was always impressed with the initiative of students who took an idea, developed a business plan, and created a profitable business for themselves. For example, one student in suburban Seattle started his own power washing business that generated more than $10,000 a year in income. Another student, in Idaho, had a passion for fishing, and she and her brother started a fishing lure business. They designed and sold their own freshwater fishing lures online and through catalogs, which developed into a lucrative venture. There are other examples of students who have developed online businesses, become Web consultants for their school system, or filled a service's niche by building a small but profitable landscaping or painting business.

Students who have to work during the term to contribute to their families' incomes are given a tremendous amount of respect in the admissions process. They're seen as the hardworking type of candidate who will be able to flourish on a campus when their term-time financial burdens are reduced. Most students choose to work part-time 5 to 10 hours a week during the school year, but admissions officers look carefully at the reasons why students might choose to work 20 or more hours per week. Is it to pay their car insurance, save for college, help with the family bills, or earn spending money for themselves? The answers to these questions can reveal an applicant's priorities and, in some circumstances, the financial pressures he or she may be experiencing. Students who work to help support their family are not expected to have significant extracurricular activities, but those who choose to work for simple monetary gain may not be adding value to the admissions application.

Working as an intern can be an outstanding learning experience, but in order for it to have more than a secondary benefit in a college application, it needs to demonstrate more responsibility than filing papers or working as part of a marketing street team. Many students who have participated in an internship are recipients of parental networking or other connections, which somewhat diminishes the importance of such an internship—especially one that is unpaid. It does not matter whether the internship is at a biotech firm or at a finance company; the value of the experience and how it influences the candidate is what concerns admissions offices.

Social Service and Community Involvement

Service is the norm rather than the exception in a high school application today. Volunteerism and community service show themselves in many ways, and the activities with which students have chosen to participate are truly amazing. Whether it's tutoring fellow students, joining a club at school, or volunteering within the community, there are ample opportunities to get involved. Service is an activity that anyone can do, and students are not dependent upon a school organization to participate. While many applicants demonstrate a penchant for a non-service-related activity that might limit their schedules, most applicants still find time to engage in community service.

With myriad opportunities available, admissions offices are interested in discovering why a student got involved with a particular organization or activity, and what level of commitment the student has demonstrated.

Many students will choose to take advantage of programs that already exist. There are numerous local and regional organizations for interested students to join, including programs offered by the school. The latter, which might take place within the school, could be a local chapter of a larger organization; other activities might be specific to the school and the local community. The level of commitment for national programs such as the Key Club, SADD, or Habitat for Humanity, which allow students to get involved within the school community, can vary from school to school. There are schools in which the service requirement is as simple as attending one meeting.

The National Honor Society is a perfect example of the possible extremes. Some schools simply hold the minimum NHS standards as the criteria for admission into the organization, while other schools add hours of service and require the elected officers to develop and implement community service programs for its members. It can be tough for admissions officers to determine just how rigorous the hours of commitment are to a particular service organi-

zation, so it's important that an applicant highlight those organizations where the selection depends upon a concerted and regular
commitment.

> **TIP:** *If you're part of a school or community organization*
> *that requires a regular and committed effort to remain a mem-*
> *ber, be sure to highlight those rigorous expectations.*

Some students have a passion for a program or an organization that
is not recognized on the school campus, so they choose to sponsor
events for that cause or create an organization within the school to
provide regular support. In recent years, diversity and cultural organizations have been founded in a large number of school districts.
Other enterprising students become involved in service through the
community rather than the school, which organizations such as the
Boys and Girls Scouts of America, Boys and Girls Clubs of America, or the local YMCA facilitate. Some may choose to make an impact through their religious community as a seminary leader, a
Bible study participant, or as religious teacher to children. Still others volunteer at day care centers, hospitals, and local women's shelters. Regardless of what you choose to do in terms of giving your
time, it's important to admissions offices that you're genuinely interested in serving others.

Candidates who use their can-do attitude to help others can lead
at the grassroots level too. A couple of brothers from Highland
Park, Illinois, decided to make a contribution to the homeless shelters in urban Chicago by collecting the food and beverages from
restaurants and stores in their affluent suburban community that
would otherwise have been thrown away. They started an organization and recruited a handful of students from the school to help run
this nightly program. This type of small but meaningful effort

demonstrates character, true commitment, and a selfless attitude that will impress any admissions committee.

Ultimately, becoming president of the school chapter of Amnesty International is not as important as the difference the organization has made in the lives of those it impacts. When it comes to service organizations, it's quite common to find applicants who join an activity and hardly become involved in the organization. It can be seen when an admissions officer peruses an application with a laundry list of activities without a sense of passion about any of them. Another disconcerting practice of less committed applicants is creating an organization in order to anoint oneself a "founder and president." Trust me when I tell you that listing these hollow activities will not help in the selective college admissions process.

> **TIP:** *Creating a new organization or a new publication can highlight initiative, but EC organizations are evaluated based on the time commitment, the amount of teamwork involved, the frequency of participation, and the volume of participation. Your application needs to show these traits in your most important activities.*

Impact of Athletics in Admission

Sports are no less an integral part of the fabric of society at the collegiate level than at the professional level. Nationally ranked athletic programs appear at leading academic institutions, such as Stanford, Duke, Northwestern, Notre Dame, and the University of Virginia, to name a few. Sports are also important to the Ivy League schools, which can produce perennial athletic powers in a handful of sports like squash, crew, lacrosse, soccer, and women's ice hockey. Individual athletes have also had success at Ivy schools and gone on to successful professional and Olympic careers. Different Ivy League sports teams will periodically rise in stature in the national scene of Division I athletics for short periods of time. Although sports have had a large influence on universities across the country, athletic recruiting in the Ivy Leagues has had the added challenge of working within the academic standards of its highly selective institutions. The admission of recruited athletes is one of the more highly scrutinized facets of the admissions process, along with the role of minority admissions, yet it may be one of the more misunderstood areas of admissions.

Some academicians challenge whether student-athletes at Ivy League schools are truly "students" and reflective of the student bodies of which they are a part. To some, success in the classroom and success in athletics are incompatible, and therefore Ivy League schools should reduce the significance of athletics in admissions. So let me admit before engaging in this debate that I played a varsity sport at Harvard and I coached there for five years. And I believe that having sports teams that can compete at the Division I level and occasionally compete nationally has been important to the health of the Ivy institutions, though I'll admit that this assertion is difficult to quantify.

Without presenting a statistical argument for athletics at the Ivies, there are a number of empirical factors that I believe are important in understanding the importance of competitive varsity athletic programs in college. Ivy League institutions seek to develop future leaders in society and top talents in their areas of expertise, including athletics. Many business, education, and political leaders can trace their college extracurricular experiences back to varsity sports programs. In many ways, the evolution of athletics in our society has mirrored the age of specialization in which we live, and it makes sense that a world-class rower might choose to focus hours each day on his or her craft with the hopes of building an Olympic and/or a professional athletic career, just as a young virtuoso violinist practices hours each day in the hope of becoming a world renowned professional.

The skills that committed athletes gain in college help them succeed during their undergraduate experience and prepare them for life after college. Ivy League athletes have gone on to successful professional careers in law, business, medicine, and education. Others have gone on to managerial and coaching positions in professional and college sports organizations or have chosen to teach and coach aspiring student athletes in high school. Some of the most financially successful and loyal alumni donors have strong connections to the varsity athletic programs they were a part of in college.

It also should be noted that many world-class athletes also want a world-class education. Without nationally competitive athletics in the Ivy League, the number of highly qualified students who choose to attend institutions like Stanford, Notre Dame, the University of North Carolina, Michigan, and U.C. Berkeley—with SAT I scores of 1400 or more and ranked in the top 5 percent of their high school class—would increase dramatically. Imagine trying to recruit a world-class cellist without a professor to act as a mentor and without an orchestra.

Every school in the Ivy League has a graduation rate above 90 percent over the past ten years, according to NCAA data, which means they have continued to maintain the benchmark of excellence for which they are known. This is significant because the Ivy graduation rates stand out when compared to other selective schools that do not emphasize nationally competitive athletics. The reports are all the more impressive because these schools' athletic programs can represent 10 to 20 percent of a given graduating class, depending on the school.

Ivy League athletics include a wide range of Division I sports, ranging from the 28 Division I men's and women's teams at Columbia to the 41 men's and women's programs at Harvard. In order to understand the nuances involved in the recruitment and the admittance of varsity athletes, there are a few general points to note.

First, many athletes are recruited by coaches each year, who attempt to identify the most talented athletes with the best chance for admission. And every year there are plenty of student-athletes who are not admitted though they were heavily recruited by coaching staffs. Second, not all Division I athletic programs receive the same amount of support or emphasis within the athletic department or in the admissions process. And finally, admissions offices pay close attention to the academic match and fit for applicants interested in playing varsity sports.

Although there are no minimum academic criteria for admissions to any of the Ivy schools for any applicant, the Ivy League has created a formula called the Academic Index, which works as a numeric guide for comparing all applicants. The AI is most often applied in the evaluation of athletes, and in some cases will act as a minimum set of academic standards for the handful of cases each year that are on the academic edge for admission.

Athletic Priorities

The number of athletes recruited in the Ivy League each year reflects an impressive commitment to varsity athletics. At most Ivy schools, these athletes have a higher matriculation rate than the general student body, in part because they've built relationships with coaches who made them feel a part of the school. By effectively building relationships with student-athletes, coaches create an attractive and inviting environment to applicants, who in turn are more likely to attend the school once they have been accepted.

Ivy schools with fewer Division I programs admit and matriculate fewer recruited athletes. At six of the eight the Ivy League schools, about 10 percent of total admissions spaces are offered to candidates who were also recruited athletes. The two Ivies with larger populations, Cornell and Penn, admit a larger raw number of student-athletes, but it represents a smaller proportion of the class.

Since admissions spots are so coveted, and because admissions offices work closely with university administrators and the athletic department to determine how much emphasis should be placed on athletics, each school makes choices about the extent to which individual sports are emphasized within the framework of particular admissions guidelines that apply to all eight Ivy League institutions. But the various schools place different emphases on certain men's and women's sports, and they will get more attention from admissions staff members.

Sports that do not receive this type of admission support typically have smaller budgets and are lower priorities within the athletic departments themselves. These internal school priorities may be based on tradition, new initiatives, and/or past program success. For instance, the men's basketball teams at Penn and Princeton have dominated the Ivy League and periodically been at the forefront of the national scene. The crew programs at Brown and Harvard have had similar success nationally and internationally. The Dartmouth, Brown, and Harvard women's ice hockey teams have recently been competing for the national championship. While these sports are not the only ones at these institutions that are successful or emphasized, success breeds success, and admissions offices seek to help highly visible and winning programs maintain their league-leading status.

One of the enrollment management challenges of Ivy schools and other highly selective schools that emphasize Division I athletics is balancing the number of athletes admitted in individual sports with the total number of varsity athletes admitted in relation to an entire admission class. The more sports that a school offers, the more the admissions office must prioritize the sports and the numbers of student-athletes who will be admitted for each program. There's no minimum number of spaces for recruited student-athletes in individual sports. The problem, when there is any, concerns the maximum number. Indeed, there may well be a limit to how many recruited candidates can be offered admission in a given sport.

In addition to the grand athletic admission scheme, each institution works to evaluate the credentials and accomplishments of each student-athlete. The Council of the Ivy presidents has long required that student-athletes be representative of the undergraduate student bodies, and the Ivy League uses the numeric AI formula to help compare student-athletes' academic credentials to the general student body within each school. The individual applicant is measured within the context of the entire applicant pool for almost all sports; however, based on the AI, football, men's basketball, and men's ice hockey have more stringent evaluation systems. Academically, the candidate is first compared to the entire pool, and then a ceiling is placed upon the number of athletes in each sport who can be admitted each year.

High-Priority Sports

Each school determines which programs will receive a high-priority status, which implies that the admissions office will make a concerted effort to admit recruited athletes who meet the admission criteria in order to help these programs field competitive teams within the Ivy League. Depending upon the needs of the program, the relationship the coach has built with the admissions office, and the qualifications of the candidates, Admissions may seek to help improve the depth of a team by offering admission to more recruited athletes and/or by focusing on the admission of one or two "program makers" within the sport. While high-priority sports will differ at each school, some Division I programs like football and basketball are given a high-priority status at all of them.

Coaches actively support a number of student-athletes each year, and if the admissions office determines that the candidate can handle the academic workload and will be a positive personal addition on campus, every effort will be made to admit this applicant. With this type of support, the key sports for each school can recruit for depth and top talents, but coaches need a keen eye for assessing that talent since they may not be able to replenish their teams at the same level each year.

Given the competition for athletes in the general admissions pool, it can be difficult for an admissions office to annually strengthen the depth of a particular team. Lacrosse, for example, has the second largest team size in the NCAA after football, but it might be two or three years before a lacrosse program will see more than seven or eight student-athletes admitted to a single class. Although high-priority sports will be able to recruit for candidates nationally, the margin for error is smaller when competing for highly selective admissions spaces outside the athletic realm. During my five years, I saw a number of recruited athletes who were great kids and weren't admitted due to the overall competition. During the last few weeks of the admissions process in particular, student-athletes are rigorously compared within the national pool, and a field hockey recruit may be bypassed for an Intel semifinalist or a class president.

Competition within the league also fosters competition within admissions. Schools may have their own lists of sports each year that are going to receive more support. A new coach may need to begin his or her coaching tenure with a large recruiting class, while another school may be committed to continuing its longstanding dominance in a particular sport. The deans of admission at the Ivy schools have a competitive spirit that permeates the entire selection process as they seek to admit the best mathematicians, the best musicians, and the best athletes wherever possible.

Coaches in high-priority and high-budget sports programs begin identifying potential student-athletes in their sophomore year. However, many coaches get their first glimpse of a student-athlete's ability through communication from high school coaches and alumni, and coaches now spend more time identifying athletes through scouting in the field. Thus, it can be beneficial for a student-athlete to market his talents to coaches prior to his or her senior year. Especially at Ivy programs that have smaller recruiting budgets, it's incumbent for prospective student-athletes to be in contact with coaches to make their athletic and academic talents known. Track and field coaches, for example, can do a better job of advocating on behalf of candidates when they receive early and accurate information about their time in the 100 meter as well as the athlete's academic standing.

TIP: *All-League/All-State caliber athletes should write to coaches prior to junior and/or senior year, listing their athletic achievements and academic credentials, which could help promote a coach's interest in them.*

For some sports programs, the significance of athletic ability may be less significant in the admissions process. With men's and women's fencing, golf, sailing, skiing, and water polo—programs that generally do not receive a tremendous amount of attention—athletes have to be exceptionally strong academically or offer more than the academic and athletic match in order to solidify their standing. As a whole, admissions offices expect these student-athletes to bring more to the campus than their athletic prowess.

Within the Ivy League, there's also a focus on revenue-generating sports programs and women's athletics. Admissions offices need to be especially responsive and sensitive to the issues that impact these athletic programs, while continuing to hold these sports to admissions standards that are applicable to each institution. The traditional revenue-generating sports at the NCAA level—men's football, basketball, and ice hockey—have the biggest recruiting budgets, and, except for Ivy League football, can be notable revenue generators for the university should an exceptional team qualify for NCAA tournament play.

The focus on these sports does not mean that Ivy League schools are not interested in non-revenue-generating sports. In fact, the opposite is true since most Ivy schools are far above the national average in the number of Division I programs per institution. The Ivy League pays close attention to revenue sports in order to ensure that these programs abide by the high academic standards set by each of these extremely selective schools. Again, the AI has been the methodology that Ivy admissions offices have used to measure the class rank and test scores of athletic applicants to their institutions relative to AI for the entire applicant pool. It has also helped establish leaguewide standards applicable at the university level for all sports.

Title IX and Women's Athletics

In 1972 the federal government created Title IX to protect against educational discrimination based on gender. The law states:

> No person in the United States shall, on the basis of sex, be
> excluded from participation in, be denied the benefits of,
> or be subject to discrimination under any education program
> or activity receiving federal financial assistance.[1]

In 1991 this law was put to the test on the athletic front by students from Brown University. Brown had decided to cut its women's gymnastics and volleyball teams, and was challenged under Title IX. The university was found not to be in compliance with Title IX legislation, and federal appeals courts since then have consistently upheld that ruling. As a result, universities are now required to provide a "substantial proportionality" standard of female student-athletes to the school's female population, and athletic departments have developed implementation plans to better serve women's collegiate sports.

In the summer of 1998, *Cohen v. Brown* was settled out of court, and Brown agreed to a proportional standard that would keep the number of female athletes to total athletes at the university within 3.5 percent of the female undergraduate student population. In addition, a number of women's programs were also elevated to varsity status.[2]

Today, alongside the focus given to men's football, basketball, and hockey, women's athletic programs garner a tremendous amount of support and attention in the admissions process. Ivy League admissions offices have been looking to support female athletics, and the opportunities for female athletes to gain admission to an Ivy League school has dramatically increased in the past ten years. *Sports Illustrated for Women* has recognized Harvard and Princeton in recent years as Top 20 schools for women who play sports, and there now may well be more women's than men's Ivy League athletic programs capable of being nationally competitive.

The academic profiles of recruited female athletes are very similar to those of male athletes, and in some cases the opportunity to build a program with talent and depth may be greater for female athletics. Field hockey, lacrosse, ice hockey, crew, and squash programs have all produced national champions from the women's ranks in the past few years at Penn, Princeton, Harvard, and Brown.

Implications of the Academic Index

The exposure sport receives in the media and in today's society lead some observers to question whether the athletes at Ivy League schools are representative of the general student body. In response, Ivy schools developed a formula to measure a candidate's quantifiable academic credentials: the Academic Index. As mentioned previously, the AI is a numeric system for evaluating student-athletes in comparison to the larger applicant pool. Using this system, admissions offices can maintain academic standards by creating an academic floor. If a particular candidate falls below that floor, the school must offer a compelling nonathletic reason to justify admission. Neither the method nor the admissions standards for athletes has changed significantly in the past decade, and the graduation rates of Ivy League students continue to remain among the highest in the nation. In fact, more students graduated with honors from Harvard in 2001—nearly 91 percent of the graduating class—than in any previous year.[3] Others forget that the Ivy League was originally formed in the nineteenth century as a sports league and has a long-standing tradition of athletic excellence.

While there's certainly been an evolution in the type of athletes who return to campus each September, athletics is still a vibrant part of the Ivy League community. The evolution of the Ivy athlete in some ways mirrors that of sports in society, while also mirroring the recent movement in American culture toward specialization. The ideal of the "liberal arts" athlete who played multiple sports and participated in numerous extracurricular activities has nearly vanished. Likewise, young musicians focus their attention on perfecting their musical abilities, debaters have chosen to master one genre of competition, and more students enter college each year with a focused academic interest.

Calculating the AI. The AI is a numeric score based on a student's average SAT I or Composite ACT score, class rank, and average SAT II subject test scores. Coaches and many high school counselors know how to calculate a student's AI. Each component is given a score between 20 and 80 points, which is similar to the scoring scale used in the SAT and simply drops the last zero from the score. There are two ways in which the formula can be generated. *Formula A.* If the average SAT I (best verbal and best math scores) or the converted Composite ACT score is higher than the average of the three highest SAT II scores, then the SAT I/ACT score will be doubled and added to the class rank score.

AI = [SAT (best verbal) + SAT (best math) ÷ 2] +
[SAT (best verbal) + SAT (best math) ÷ 2] + class rank score

Formula B. If a candidate's three highest SAT II scores are higher than the SAT I/ACT average, then the formula is calculated by adding the average SAT I (best verbal and best math scores) or the converted Composite ACT with the average of the three highest SAT II exams and with the class rank score.

AI = [SAT (best verbal) + SAT (best math) ÷ 2] +
[SAT II + SAT II + SAT II ÷ 3] + class rank score

The highest possible score for the AI is 240, which would represent a student with an 800 verbal and 800 math SAT (80 + 80 ÷ 2
= 80); a class rank score of 80, which is given to applicants who are
first in a class of 300 or more students; a GPA of 4.3 and above, or
a percentage average of 98 and above at schools that do not provide
absolute rank.

Every student admitted to an Ivy League university has a calculated AI, though in nonathletic cases it is rarely looked at as part of
the admissions decision-making process. Each year, the AI average
is calculated for each of the Ivy schools, and this average becomes
the baseline for athletic admissions for each school. The average
AI for all athletes admitted to each of the Ivy institutions must fall
within one standard deviation of the entire admitted class from the
previous year, and only a handful of athletes each year can be admitted with an AI greater than 2.5 of a standard deviation from the
class AI average. The concept behind this formula ensures that almost all the athletes will academically fall within the distribution
curve that is representative of the school's entire student body.

The average AI scores for the entire student body for each of the
Ivy schools can be broken down into two tiers, with Dartmouth,
Harvard, Princeton, and Yale having higher AI average range requirements than Brown, Columbia, Cornell, and Penn. These university AI averages correlate closely with the average SAT range
and class rank of the entire student bodies at each institution. A student with higher standardized scores can afford to have a slightly
lower class rank and still maintain a strong AI, and students with
lower standardized test scores will have to perform at a high level in
the classroom in order to remain a strong candidate.

To have an AI near the average of most Ivy schools' student bodies, a candidate needs an SAT I of about 1350 and should rank in the top 5 percent of his or her class. For example, a student with a 1350 SAT I with an A– average, and ranked 14 out of 400, would have an AI around 206 (135 for the SAT + 71 for class rank score). (For teachers, coaches, parents, and students interested in knowing a candidate's AI, see the Appendix for the converted rank score tables to determine one's class rank score, which can be applied to the AI formula.)

Small School Students at a Disadvantage. The AI is affected by schools with graduating classes below 300 students. In fact, the converted rank scores (CRS) assigned to students at these small schools when calculating an AI prohibits top achieving students from being given appropriate credit for high academic achievement. For example, a student who graduates first in a class of 100 students can only receive a converted rank score of 76 points, while the valedictorian in a class of 150 receives 77 points, and in a class of 250 would receive 79 points.

Every year very good student-athletes at smaller schools may be put at a disadvantage through no fault of their own. I don't believe a student should be denied the maximum benefit when they've produced at the maximum level. Until this minor glitch in the system is addressed, I would encourage guidance counselors at smaller schools to advocate that Ivy admissions staffs reevaluate the system so that it will provide maximum benefit to the valedictorian, salutatorians, and other high-achieving students who are limited by their class size and not their talents.

Lower Limit Range. In addition to being a schoolwide standard to measure athletic recruits against the entire class, the AI also sets a lower limit range. It falls somewhere greater than 2.5 standard deviations from the class average to the lower limit AI average. This number can periodically change, since it reflects the collaborative decisions of the Ivy League based upon all of the schools' AI averages. The total number of student athletes admitted in the lower academic index range depends upon the school, but the rough estimate of spaces offered in this range each year is about 1 to 2 percent of the total number of admissions.

The 20 or so student-athletes admitted in this range each year are considered carefully for the academic "match" and are discussed at great length in each of the schools' admissions committees. Student-athletes whose academic credentials fall in this range are highly rated athletes with All-League, Olympic, or professional potential, according to the coaching staffs. In most of the cases, it was low SAT scores that lowered the AI average, while a handful of these candidates may have had slightly higher scores combined with a middling transcript. International student-athletes with a low verbal score and students from small, rural districts or poor urban schools with limited offerings are not uncommon examples of these applicants.

At Harvard, the admissions committee tries to measure the tangible and intangible traits of these candidates in order to get a sense of whether they have the necessary attributes for achieving academic success. Do they have the "fire in the belly" to work hard in the classroom? Teacher recommendations, course selection, interviews, and grades are leading indicators. Do candidates understand the academic challenges that await them at a place where they may find academic success difficult? Does the individual candidate have the skills necessary to pass what is colloquially called the "broken leg test": Would he or she be an asset to the campus if unable to play the sport due to injury or other circumstance? The last two questions are often drawn from the personal interview with the candidate.

Before making an affirmative decision, we always sought to meet, in person, a student-athlete whose academic credentials fell at one end of the academic distribution curve. The "broken leg test" in particular was something that our committee weighed heavily as we tried to ensure that our student-athletes would be a good fit in all facets of college life. For candidates who may find academic life challenging, it's even more important to be the type of person who asks for help from tutoring resources when necessary, and to be the kind of person who finds success and happiness in a school even if one couldn't for some reason play the sport. For a student who meets these standards, the admissions committee is more inclined to take a calculated risk on a great athlete.

Coaches and the AI. The AI also plays a somewhat more prominent role in admissions for the revenue-generating sports mentioned earlier. Only football and men's basketball and ice hockey actually have to work within a defined process when calculating the AI of their prospective student-athletes. These sports must work within set limitations that define the number of admittances and matriculating student-athletes each year. In addition, these programs are also required to recruit set numbers of student-athletes within AI ranges or to calculate an AI composite average for the entire team. The coaches have the added responsibility of identifying a larger pool of qualified academic candidates than other sports, insofar as the coaching staffs will be limited to a set number of candidates who might be admitted, regardless of how strong the academic credentials of the candidates might be.

Though the AI plays an insignificant role for most athletes interested in Ivy athletics, for some coaches it's the most decisive element in their recruiting. After all, athletic recruiting is a joint process in which coaches and admissions offices work together to admit the best student-athletes who will both compete for Ivy League championships and flourish in the classroom, and the AI is a way for admissions offices to give coaches guidance in terms of where a student-athlete stands academically. After coaches identify how talented a prospective athlete is and how good the athlete might be in college, they provide the admissions office with a priority list of student-athletes whom they would most like to have admitted. Admissions officers then look into the academic match, the personal qualities, and the other factors that influence admissions decisions for all candidates. These factors are measured with the needs of the sport and in the context of the entire applicant pool, and admissions decisions are made accordingly.

What an Athletic Candidate Needs to Do

If you're a student-athlete or the parent of an athlete interested in playing varsity athletics at a highly selective school, consider the following general points. They can help you understand the relationship between your grades and your athletics.

- Contact the coaches in the sport(s) you're interested in playing in college by writing a letter that highlights your athletic and academic accomplishments. Include a season schedule and your coach's contact information. If a coach believes you can make an impact on their team, he or she will become your strongest advocate.

- Coaches at highly selective schools need to know your grades and test scores in addition to your athletic accomplishments, so include your academic credentials in any communications.

- If your test scores are lower than you would like, retaking standardized tests can only help your AI. Good grades can, to a small extent, offset low scores.

- Absolute rank: Students who attend smaller high schools (smaller than 250 in size) may be negatively impacted by the AI, which prohibits a good student from receiving the maximum allotted point total in the class rank score.

- Calculating the AI: This number is crucial for a handful of sports or for students whose standardized test scores or rank are lower than most students in the applicant pool. Contact a coach to understand more about the importance of the AI in a specific sport, and use the formula listed in this chapter and in the Appendix to determine your Academic Index.

- High-priority sports recruit at the national level and spend significant dollars trying to identify and encourage student-athletes to apply. They have identified nearly all of their recruits prior to December of that recruiting year.

- Some high-priority sports like crew, cross-country, and track and field rely heavily on referral and first contact from interested student-athletes. Every year, a few applicants are identified late in the process as top athletes by coaches.

- Low-priority sports have a smaller recruiting budget, and coaches need to rely more on candidates who apply to the university and show an interest in the sport than on an aggressive recruiting system that encourages juniors and seniors in high school to apply.

Recognized Extracurricular Programs and Positions

Table 3-1 reviews top-tier extracurricular programs and scholarships as seen by admissions committees. It is by no means a com-

Table 3-1 *Sample Levels of Involvement in*
Extracurricular Activities (National and Regional Programs)

Type or Genre	Name(s) of National Program(s) or Example	Highly Recognized Leadership Positions, Awards within Program
Politics and Government	Boys and Girls Nation	President, Vice President, Attorney General
Politics and Government	Boys and Girls State	Governor, Lt. Governor, Attorney General, State Senator
Politics and Government	U.S. Senate Youth Program	
Politics and Government	U.S. Senate Page School	
Politics and Government	Statewide Student Government Associations	Officer positions
Debate	NFL and CFL National Tournament	Category National Champion, Semifinalist
Music	National Concerto Competition	
Performing Arts	National Ballet/Dance Programs (such as the Boston Ballet)	Dancer in *Nutcracker*, etc.
Music	Grammy High School Jazz Ensemble	
Music	National Youth Symphony Orchestra	Concertmaster, 1st chair
Performing Arts	Professional Acting	Television, Screen, Broadway
Service	Future Farmers of America	National President
Scholarship	Wendy's Heisman Award	National Winner
Scholarship	Bronfman Youth Scholars	25 national awards

Type or Genre	Regional/State Programs	Highly Recognized Leadership Positions, Awards
Politics and Government	Associated Student Body Government	President and other officer positions
Politics and Government	Student Representative to the School Board or Principal's Advisory Board	
Politics and Government	Class Officer	
Politics and Government	Model Congress/Model UN Conference at U Chicago, Harvard, UC Berkeley, etc.	Best Delegate Award
Music	Interlochen, Tanglewood Summer Music Program	
Music	All-State Band	
Music	All-State Choir/Vocal	
Music	Select Youth Symphony Orchestras	Concertmaster, 1st chair
Service, other	4-H	Regional Officer
Service, other	Future Farmer's of America	Regional Officer
Service	Boy Scouts	Eagle Scout
Service	Girl Scouts	Gold/Silver Award
Service	Key Club	President
Service	National Honor Society	President
Publications/ Writing	School Newspaper	Editor in Chief, Section Editor
Publications/ Writing	School Yearbook	Editor in Chief
Publications/ Writing	NCTE Writing Award	
Scholarship	ROTC Scholarship	
Religious	LDS Seminary School	Seminary President
Service, Cultural	Jack and Jill	Regional Officer

plete list of programs, but it will give you a sense of some activities that annually receive the highest recognition. Students whose preferred activities and participant organizations are not listed, but who may have a comparable commitment or local recognition, should ask their mentors and advisers to impress that commitment upon the admissions committee.

The *National* designation, referring to a nationally competitive position or award, has the highest value in the applicant pool. *Regional* refers to programs, awards, and positions that tend to be more locally focused. All of these programs carry significant weight in the admissions process, but the regional programs may not be as distinguishable from other outstanding programs that have a similarly strong basis within their national region.

Extracurricular Profile of Students Admitted to Highly Selective Colleges

While there are many interesting paths in which a student can travel in the extracurricular world, admissions officers are able to categorize common themes and attributes that stand out in the profile of an applicant to a highly selective college. Listed below are high-level profiles of how various "types" of applicants might be categorized for their ECAs during the evaluation process.

Nationally Recognized: Heavily Recruited Talents

- These students are recognized nationally or internationally for their talents. They are specialists and may be engaged in fewer activities aside from their specialized skill(s). These candidates have a clear distinguishing excellence, "D.E." in admissionsspeak.

- They are musicians, athletes, actors/actresses, dancers, debaters, and the most highly acclaimed student leaders in the country, recognized as such through organizations, competitions, or other notable programs.

- A percentage of these candidates will be heavily recruited athletes. Anywhere from 6 to 15 percent of total admissions at Ivy League schools will be recruited athletes in both male and female varsity programs.

- These students may have attended Boys or Girls Nation or other leadership programs based on a competitive selection process.

- They are nationally recruited musicians who most likely have won national concerto competitions or been identified by music faculty members.

- A handful of these students will have had child/teen roles in television, the movies, or Broadway-type theater.

- Some in this category have won national competitions in debate, film, art, vocal performance, or service, while a few each year will have shown uncommon entrepreneurship, commitment to public service, or creativity that is evaluated by admissions officers as equally strong to other works they've seen in this category in previous years.

- These candidates are often evaluated as "best in career" or "as good as anyone in the last five to ten years" by teachers, mentors, and coaches.

A Solid Extracurricular Hook: Strong Regional and Local Candidates

- This is the largest group of admitted candidates to highly selective schools, representing the majority of admitted students. They are often referred to as the "high-level, all-around" candidates.

- They do many things well, are leaders in a number of areas within their community, and are exceptional in one or two areas—though their skills are not recognized at the national level, they have an exceptional balance of depth and breadth of activity.

- They have been elected to significant leadership positions within their school and possibly region. They are student body presidents, Eagle Scouts, Girls State attendees, multisport captains, and newspaper editors in chief.

- They have been drama leads, won NCTE awards, been student representatives to the school board, and have been instrumental within their school and community.

- They are noticeably involved in service programs, religious organizations, cultural activities, or other organizations.

- The letters of recommendation identify these candidates as the most promising leaders in the applicant pool, "the best this year."

The Well-Rounded Candidate May Lack a Hook or "Distinguishing Excellence"

- A small percentage of candidates fall into this category. They invariably have strengths outside the extracurricular realm of regional and national acclaim—typically in the areas of academics and personal qualities.

- These candidates participate in two or more activities but lack the distinction of many of their peers. Some might be classified as followers rather than leaders in the extracurricular realm.

- Although these candidates may not be distinguished in these areas, they truly enjoy their activities. They are not engaged in clubs or organizations simply for the purpose of building a résumé.

Circumstances That Limit Extracurricular Involvement

Candidates who find themselves limited to participate in extracurricular activities due to personal or family circumstances are not placed at a disadvantage in the admissions process. Students from modest financial backgrounds who need to work during the school year in order to financially support themselves or their families are not required to have amassed the same EC portfolio that others may have put together. In fact, candidates who work 20 hours a week or more are typically given the same type of credit for work as they would for spending those hours on a sports team or in a musical group. Students heavily involved in helping raise their siblings because of parental work commitments or other extenuating circumstances are also not held to the same EC standard.

And finally, admissions committees also recognize and take into account applicants who have physical disabilities that limit participation in extracurricular activities. In accordance with federal laws and national standards, admissions offices look at the performance and success of candidates who are unable participate in extracurricular activities due to a disability without prejudice.

Endnotes

1. Title IX, Education Amendment (Title 20 U.S.C. Chapter 38: Sex, Section: 1681). The Title IX Amendment can also be found at the Department of Labor Web site at www.dol.gov/oasam/regs/statutes/titleix.htm (July 2002).
2. "Judge Approves Settlement of Brown U.'s Title IX Case," *The Chronicle of Higher Education*, July 3, 1998.
3. Patrick Healy, "Harvard's Honors Fall to the Merely Average," *The Boston Globe*, October 8, 2001.

PERSONAL QUALITIES AND BACKGROUND FACTORS IMPACT ON THE APPLICATION

As colleges and universities aspire to be a microcosm of the society and the communities in which they're located, they seek to enroll a student body that is a well-rounded cross section of the world. To this end, admissions offices search for applicants with exceptional character and leadership potential. Not only are these traits critical for fostering an enriching intellectual campus environment and for producing future leaders, but through the measurement of personal qualities admissions offices distinguish truly extraordinary people from the many applicants who are accomplished on paper.

The search to select leaders with outstanding character draws from all parts of the globe, applicants with a wide range of interests and from a multitude of cultural, geographic, socioeconomic, religious, and ethnic backgrounds. This approach is in accord with the belief among many educators that the learning opportunities available to university students outside the classroom or laboratory are as important as what is learned inside the classroom. Learning from peers who share their unique backgrounds, interests, and experiences creates a stimulating environment that influences students' lives during and after college. By understanding demographic, environmental, and individual factors that round out an application, admissions officers can examine the intangible factors that "add value" to a campus that is based on the individual qualities of the applicant. The sum of these qualities, of course, will add to the campus dynamic.

In this chapter we'll focus on personal qualities while outlining the key components of the application that impact admissions decisions. At the same time, we'll present an overview of some intangible factors that influence admissions committees, and we'll discuss the manner in which admissions staffs look at the directions prospective students might possibly take after graduation.

Why Personal Character Is Important

The most qualitative component of the admissions process is the assessment of personal character. It's also the element that reveals a more complete picture of the candidate than the quantitative components alone can provide.

As a hiring manager conducts an interview to evaluate a potential employee's fit for a job, admissions staffs look not only at a candidate's quantitative abilities, but take personal and other intangible factors presented in the application into account, such as background. Just as a hiring manager needs a keen sense for the qualities that will lead to success within a company, an admissions officer must have a discerning eye and an appreciation for the appealing and unique personal characteristics that presage success in college. The application often provides readers with information that highlights a candidate's maturity, passion or depth or strength of character. In addition, an application can unveil the fine character, integrity, or leadership qualities that might become an important factor in choosing from a number of high-caliber candidates.

Sometimes the information revealed about a candidate can be subtle, such as whether the candidate's parents attended college. In other cases, it might be immediately apparent that an applicant's experience has a significant impact, such as how he or she handled or is presently coping with a difficult health issue. As the admissions cycle evolves, a reader will learn more about the candidate with each subsequent review of the folder, with new insights into the individual each time the application is perused. In assessing personal qualities, the value of the application materials is enormous, enabling committee members to make well-informed judgments about the candidates seeking admission.

The melding of passionate, introspective, quirky, and gregarious individuals add to the quality of life on a university campus. What clearly defines men and women of outstanding accomplishment and character, however, becomes less clear when an admissions office tries to define the profile of the student body. Students who attend highly selective institutions conform to no one specific personality type, but we can generalize and present the following personality profiles—three broad categories of candidates who seem to represent a large portion of each year's newly admitted class.

The All-Around Candidate

I use the term "all-around candidate" only in the sense that these applicants have a wide range of substantive traits that have made them successful throughout high school and will probably serve them similarly well in the future. This candidate, representing a majority of the students admitted to highly selective schools, displays the outgoing, charming, and engaging personality needed to be successful and to be a leader.

These individuals are affable, gregarious, tend to show more maturity than their peers, and are passionate about their interests and beliefs. They typically present themselves very well in interviewing situations. I might also call them "all-American candidates" because they're the ones whose recommendations from teachers and interviewers include statements like, "I only hope my daughter/son can grow up to be like . . ."

These applicants are both personable and substantial. They have a genuine concern for others, they want to make a difference in their community or world, and they're energized by a stimulating university setting. They do what they do because they simply enjoy it. Their interests are broad, and the life choices they'll make help them to learn more about themselves and better prepare them for the future. For an admissions officer, these candidates are often referred to as the kind of applicant you'd like to have as a roommate or as a friend in college.

While many of the admitted students will have appealing personal skills, strong character and charm can make a difference when choosing among all of the talented candidates. Every year there are some great all-around candidates whose personal traits carry them to the finish line.

Consider, for example, the class valedictorian from a high school in the Santa Fe, New Mexico area, who had a 1400 range on the SAT I and whose SAT II scores ranged from 800 to 760 to a 570. Her strong extracurricular activities included community service, a term-time job, martial arts, and an all-state music level. But her admission was still in doubt. It was the school's support, which characterized her as a terrific person who was among the best candidates to ever apply to a highly selective college from that high school. The glowing interview with a Harvard alumnus added to the application, and together with the positive support led to a positive result when the admissions committee made its final decisions in March.

The Focused and Driven Candidate

There are plenty of students accepted at highly selective institutions who can be classified as very focused individuals. They're bright, with an intensely clear vision of who they are and what they want in their lives. These students fare well in an interview setting because they can articulate their personal, academic, and career goals in a meaningful way, and they are clearly positively motivated. They're also goal oriented and have enormous drive.

Much of the competitiveness that characterizes this type comes from an internal driving force that directs them to great achievements. For some, the internal drive comes from parental pressure; others are self-motivated to be the best; and for still others the motivation to succeed may come from the fear of failure or other life lessons that have taught them to push hard toward a goal. Whatever the source of their drive, these candidates have well-laid plans for their college experience and will maximize the utility of college life. Many will go on to have very successful professional careers.

Admissions officers will look closely for maturity and perspective from these applicants in order to avoid admitting an overly focused candidate who runs the risk of burnout or is unable to cope with the challenges or adversity one may encounter in college. Many graduates of highly selective schools who have successfully entered the professional world could be categorized as highly focused undergraduates with a pronounced perspective on life.

The Quietly Substantive Candidate

The personal qualities of more reserved candidates can be elusive. These applicants, who may be the brightest intellects on campus, often tend to be more reserved in an interview setting and around those with whom they're less familiar. Though thoughtful and substantial, their reserved nature may keep their depth from shining through.

In the university setting they tend to gravitate to smaller social circles and/or display a singular focus. It's not uncommon for this type to have a more difficult time adjusting to college and life away from home for the first time. From a personal perspective, these candidates have the biggest up side: As they mature and "come out of their shell," their impact on the campus becomes more pronounced.

I was an academic adviser for several students who were more reserved or contemplative and who needed time to get used to college life away from home. One of these students, from Minnesota, had a 1600 SAT I, two SAT II 800s, and nine AP scores of 5, and he was one of the most intelligent persons I advised while at Harvard. In academic settings and in his interview, he was impressive on all accounts; however, he was quieter around his peers in social settings. As he became accustomed to life at college, he blossomed, becoming involved with his peers in social and extracurricular activities. He added much to the Harvard Math Department, but also learned to use his personal skills and academic gifts to give back to others by participating in a group that taught physics principles to Cambridge youths.

Letters of Recommendation

As the pieces are put together, an interesting array of characteristics begin to surface from the applications, which develops into a complex pool of individuals who will add to the mix of the class. In addition to gaining a more complete picture of the person behind the application, readers are also on the lookout for traits that will raise concern over the possible adjustment of the applicant to the college. Is the student painfully shy or timid, aloof, or a grade grubber? What a reader can glean from the application is astounding, with the Letters of Recommendation, personal essays, and interviews the main vehicles for learning more about the qualities a candidate will bring to campus.

Although the number of reports and the specific requirements vary, most admissions offices require two teacher letters and a letter written by a high school guidance counselor. Teachers in academic subjects should write the Letters of Recommendation, and in some cases an admissions office might require an English teacher to write a letter. A candidate might be required to submit a Letter of Recommendation from a math or science teacher if he or she is applying to a School of Engineering or another math/science-related department.

From a student's perspective, it's important to ask teachers that know you well to write your letters rather than to ask teachers who have simply given you good grades to write on your behalf. The substance of these letters is always more important than who writes the letter! Faculty members who are also academic advisers, coaches, and club moderators will be able to write some of the strongest teacher letters because they've spent the most time with you during your years in high school.

Who You Are

The teacher's role in the admissions process is twofold. First, they're asked to describe more about your academic and personal qualifications. While having a teacher who can describe your mellifluous writing style or can validate your original research projects provides valuable information about your academic credentials, admissions readers would also like to know what you'll bring to college from a personal perspective.

The recommendation form starts by asking how long the teacher has known the applicant and in what classes the teacher taught him or her. It's far more valuable to ask a tenth grade teacher who knows you well to write about you than to ask a twelfth grade teacher whom you have known for less than a month. The most effective letters are those that tell readers about how you raised the level of conversation in class every day, how you made the school a better place to be, or that reveal something substantive about the teacher's personal relationship with you. The best letters present a more personal portrayal of the candidate than a detailed restatement of your transcript and extracurricular accomplishments.

How You Compare

The second element that makes a teacher Letter of Recommendation important is the comparative nature of these reports. Each recommendation form has a rating checklist of general qualities that are important to admissions officers. Teachers are asked to rate students for their intellectual curiosity, academic promise, self-confidence, warmth of personality, and concern for others, to name a few on a scale from "one of the best in my career" to "top 5 percent this year" down to "average or below." Most of the strong candidates receive high marks in the academic areas, but there can be a wide range of selections in the areas more closely related to personal character.

In addition to the checklists, comparisons in the substance of the letters are most helpful, since they can help identify elite students within an applicant pool from a single school and help compare these students to past applicants accepted to highly selective schools.

> **TIP:** *Take the time to get to know your teachers, and ask the teachers who know you best to write on your behalf. Be sure to ask them well in advance of the application deadline to give them the most time to write a well-crafted letter.*

Secondary School Report and Counselor Letter

The main purpose for the Secondary School Report (SSR) is to garner the official school transcript, class rank, information on any disciplinary matters, and any other pertinent information about the school or the candidate.

The guidance counselor letter is more dependent upon the resources and emphasis given to counseling within the school district. For schools with larger guidance staffs, counselors are able to spend more time with the students and thus can write a more comprehensive Letter of Recommendation. Private schools often invest resources in their counseling staff, and the time they spend getting to know and advocating for a candidate can add significantly to the application. Counselors in public schools with high student-to-counselor ratios—such as those in California, Nevada, Florida, and Texas—will have a more challenging time getting to know the students well and representing them adequately for highly selective colleges. For these school systems, students may be able to find a third teacher Letter of Recommendation to fulfill the application requirements.

Supplementary Letters

Applicants are also welcome to submit supplementary Letters of Recommendation. A student may wish to have an art teacher write a letter detailing the depth of the candidate's portfolio and artistic potential. A coach or a mentor might wish to talk more about an individual's contributions outside of class. Others may choose to have a university professor with whom the candidate conducted research write a letter about the quality of the candidate's work and academic promise.

When a student wants to mount a campaign, so to speak, the letters can readily flow into the admissions office. Applicants are always welcome to send in extra Letters of Recommendation, but I would advise a student to limit the total number of additional letters to two. The more supplemental Letters of Recommendation in an application, the more difficult it is for an admissions officer to decide which ones best reveal the candidate's qualities. Also, your application may not receive multiple readings, and Letters of Recommendation received more than a month after the application deadline run the risk of not being reviewed in detail.

> **TIP:** *Develop a strategy behind selecting teachers and other appropriate writers for your Letters of Recommendation:*
> 1. *Give ample time to those whom you ask to write.*
> 2. *Limit additional recommendations to the most appropriate few.*
> 3. *Try to submit all Letters of Recommendation as close to the application deadline as possible.*

How Important Are Reference Letters?

The importance of reference letters depends upon how much the admissions office knows about a school, the depth of the letter written by the teacher or counselor, or by the competitiveness of the individual applicant. If the candidate has less compelling grades, scores, and accomplishments and is therefore not developing into a contender for discussion in the committee meetings, readers will quickly skim the letters for any information that might be of significance. In addition, readers turn to the letters for more background when they are unfamiliar with the school and how the candidate contributed to the school community.

Having a good relationship with an admissions office can build real trust between the teachers and admissions staffs and have a positive impact for some candidates. At schools where I received applications each year, I did the best I could to study the letters of teachers who wrote for multiple candidates within a school. It was a good way for me to distinguish students from one another within a high school in one particular academic area. Whether a teacher clearly identified an applicant as more compelling than others or distinguished the candidates in a subtler manner, noting the comments by the same teacher on multiple applicants proved to be a valuable tool of analysis.

For those teachers who doubt the importance of their letters, an anecdote is in order. I had the misfortune of reading letters from teachers from two different high schools who wrote identical, word for word recommendations for all of their students. In both instances, these teachers undermined the credibility of their school and themselves, and the results, if not addressed, can have a negative impact on the candidates from those schools. In each case, our office wrote to these teachers voicing our concerns. In one of the cases, the teacher became an outstanding advocate for future applicants from that high school, writing especially in-depth letters.

Admissions offices also rely on the professionalism of college counselors to help identify truly special candidates. While many counselors had the ability to represent the interests of their students with the needs of our offices, I found the schools in the Chicago area to be particularly responsive when I needed more information and the straight story on a particular candidate. This type of communication paid long-term dividends for their schools because I knew that I was receiving a professional, honest, and well-balanced review of their students. I knew when the school felt very strongly about an applicant because they did not use the "best in years" designation frivolously.

Degrees of Separation: Making Recommendations and School Support Stand Out

The contents of Letters of Recommendation can have a significant impact on the outcome of an admissions decision. Most letters written about candidates are termed as "standard strong." The broad generalizations they provide about a candidate could apply to most other applicants as well.

Lisa is a hardworking, conscientious student. Bobby is a terrific person with outstanding character. Diane is a leader and a role model to her peers. While all of these are excellent qualities that selective schools expect to see in their applicants, the comments alone do not elevate the applicant's case above others. Sometimes the letters are viewed as standard strong because a teacher may be inexperienced in writing a letter for a candidate in a highly competitive applicant pool. Consider the following example of a positive letter written on behalf of a candidate that would be read as standard strong by admissions officers.

It is my pleasure to recommend Melissa Gagne to your university. Melissa is an outstanding student and leader at our high school. She has enrolled in one of the most demanding academic programs in our school and has maintained a straight A average. Her intelligence is rivaled only by her work ethic in the classroom, and she has been recognized by the faculty in the English Department for her achievements with the Senior English Award. She has two AP scores of 5 on the AP English Literature and Biology. With scores of 1410, Melissa was also recognized as National Merit Commended Scholar.

Outside of the classroom, Melissa has been heavily involved in volunteer work and student government. She was class president in grade 11, and she has recently been elected as the ASB president. In addition to politics, she is very active in community service as an officer in Interact Club and through a local homeless shelter. Melissa also plays varsity softball.

Melissa is a great person in many respects. She demonstrates exceptional leadership and personal qualities. She is focused, highly motivated, and capable, and she is respected by students and teachers alike. I am confident that Melissa will be a wonderful college student and be an asset to your college.

This mock letter offers a nice portrayal of Melissa's accomplishments. The teacher reviewed her academic credentials and extracurricular activities, but the letter does not go into details of what makes her contributions in any of those areas special. Maybe the teacher could have given a more in-depth description of her English award, and it might have been helpful to know what made her such an appealing candidate for ASB president. In personal terms, she sounds nice, but there is no real sense of an "unusual appeal" that admissions officers are trying to uncover. Reading into the letter, there may be something special about Melissa, but it's hard to know. A little more substance from the teacher could easily make Melissa's recommendation sing.

In other instances the prose may actually fit the applicant, and the teacher may see this person as strong but not necessarily a "best of" type of case. Sometimes these standard letters serve the purpose of providing intentionally muted praise. In some school systems, parents are so involved in the application process that teachers and counselors are hesitant to write anything that could be perceived as disparaging. In such instances, what teachers do not say can sometimes lead to some valuable conclusions about the candidate. Statements such as, "She is a highly competitive person with tremendous room for growth," or, "He is a person who is about to come into his own," are far from ringing endorsements of the candidate. These subtle inferences can be taken as a warning signal about a student's current level of maturity, confidence, or concern for others.

The best letters will always be personal in nature. They refer to examples of leadership rather than a list of accomplishments, and they talk about the unique characteristics that distinguish a candidate from his or her peers. In some cases the letters reveal something more telling about the candidate. Many self-effacing and modest students have their stories of personal triumph, of overcoming adversity, or of compelling interest told by their teachers. These recommendations can set apart students in terms of personal qualities. Cases that warrant the most in-depth review will also need this type of recommendation to help them rise above others, and strong school support can help build a case that might otherwise be at the edge of admission.

With such a large number of letters to read in a short window of time, admissions readers are looking for high-level key words or phrases that signal: READ ME—THIS IS IMPORTANT. These key words and phrases are comparative or superlative in nature, and they often address the candidates in terms that provide distinction. Some of them might look like:

- Elizabeth is the best student and all-around candidate in our class this year.

- Peter is one of the best athletes our school has seen in the last five years, and we sent other talented recruits to a number of Division I schools.

- Joshua is one of the top three mathematicians I have had the pleasure to teach in my career.

- Kelly is as strong a candidate as any of the students admitted from our school to your university in the last ten years.

- Rarely have I enjoyed teaching and getting to know someone as much as I have David.

- Yvonne is the first student in our school's history to attend Girls Nation.

Teachers who have the ability to write in this fashion without using hyperbole will enhance the case of an applicant. Meaningful comparisons help draw a more accurate picture of the contributions a candidate has made to her community and to draw distinctions among applicants. Such superlatives highlight the strengths of the candidate on his own, in the eyes of the teacher, in comparison to his present and past peers from his school and to the overall pool of students that come from that school. This type of letter can also help boost a candidate as a comparison to the entire applicant pool.

The Personal Essay and the Story It Tells

Almost everything that appears in the application is a compellation of data about the candidate or of comments written about the applicant by others. More often than not, the essay brings together and affirms much of what is already known about the applicant, but the additional insights into the person can be very valuable to admissions officers.

Most colleges use the fairly standard and open-ended essay topics similar to what can be found in the Common Application, a standard application accepted at more than 100 colleges and universities across the country. The essay topics do not change significantly, if at all, from year to year. Typically the candidate is asked to write about a person who has had a significant influence on them, an issue that has meaning for them, an event or experience in life that greatly impacted them, or a creative topic. "Discuss an issue of personal, local, national, or international concern and its importance to you" has been an essay question since at least 1995.

Other admissions offices will craft their own essay questions, which are designed to focus the writer on topics that may reveal more about their creativity and thought process. These essay topics can be as direct as one of the choices offered in the 2001 application at Northwestern: "In your view, what constitutes honor?" Although atypical, essays can also be thought-provoking and intellectually challenging, such as this one from the University of Chicago:

> The Sudanese author Tayeb Salih wrote, "Turning to left and right, I found I was halfway between north and south. I was unable to continue, unable to return." If he is unable to choose, the character faces the threat of being frozen in place or torn between two states. Describe a halfway point in your life—

a moment between your own kind of "north" and "south." Tell us about your choice, your inability to choose, or perhaps your folly in thinking there was ever a choice to be made.[1]

Some Cautions

The essay for some candidates weaves a story about personal achievements, experiences, and challenges that might otherwise not have been a part of the application. While an effective essay can pull a candidate's story and the application more closely together, the instances where the essay adds more than color or a complement are few and far between. Applicants who have a story that may be compelling should use the essay as a forum to share that experience; however, I would caution students and teachers to be wary of overemphasizing the importance of the college essay.

First, the essay can't replace four years of academic accomplishment. The transcript, test scores, and Letters of Recommendation will still comprise the core data, and an assessment of writing ability from the essays is secondary to the academic credentials. If an applicant's writing becomes a significant determining factor in the process, an admissions office may look to other written submissions. Newspaper articles, literary magazine submissions, original prose, and a school newspaper or award-winning piece submitted to a competition can be additional tools for examining writing skill.

Second, the increasing focus on the art of writing a "winning" college essay has seriously weakened the significance of the personal essay. This includes books such as *50 Successful Harvard Application Essays*,[2] the proliferation of essay-writing and editing services on the Internet, the growth of the private counseling industry, and the integration of college essay writing into the classroom. Some schools that I covered actually had "The College Essay" as a first semester senior English elective. Is it possible for the school and the students' motives to be any more obvious? The essay is even more vulnerable than the SAT to the plight of wealthy customers who are willing to pay resources for enhanced results. As a result, admissions officers read these essays with a healthy amount of skepticism. In some cases, an essay with rough edges indicates an effort that was more an individual than a "community" effort.

Finally, essays do not get students admitted to college. As I said before, they add a piece to the puzzle and complement the application by adding a little more personal insight that may confirm or express what is already known about the candidate. Time is a consideration as well. It takes approximately 20 to 30 minutes to read an applicant's file during the first reading of the application, and for a strong contender, it can take a reader 40 minutes or more to read and then write an assessment of the candidate. Unless there is a compelling reason to analyze or scrutinize an essay, admissions officers will spend two to three minutes at most reading the essay. Periodically, an essay that is compelling or revealing about the candidate will be read before the full committee, but fewer than 5 percent of the applicants will receive that level of attention.

Several of my admitted students' essays have been reviewed in publications and other resources outlining the strengths of the essays and how they impacted the decision-making process. I was amazed to learn that the analysts knew what I was actually thinking and how those essays impacted our admissions decisions. In fact, nearly all the examples of genuinely thoughtful essays that can be found on the Web and in various publications validate other information already provided in the application.

TIP: *Most essays will be read by one or two people. Craft a well-written story, but do not overemphasize its significance in the process. A solid, well-written essay should be your primary concern.*

As much as a revealing essay can draw a reader to take a longer look at an applicant, a poorly written essay can attract attention and raise concerns in committee meetings. If you follow some simple rules, your essay will serve its purpose and have the same impact as a polished essay reviewed and partially written by expensive editing services. I'll first state the obvious: Follow the basic rules of grammar! Admissions officers do break out the red pens in search of misplaced modifiers, poorly constructed sentences, and other grammatical errors. In our office, there were a couple of pet peeves that always raised the ire of the staff. Here's a summation:

- Familiarize yourself with the basic rules of grammar. *Myriad* for example, is an adjective and not a noun—never use *myriad of* in a sentence. *Unique* is an adjective intended to be used without qualifying modifiers. Avoid qualifying terms such as *very unique.*

- Avoid essays that read like a thesaurus, since they will not flow well and will be perceived as a poor attempt to impress readers with an SAT-like vocabulary.

- Avoid hyperbole designed for dramatic effect.

- Be wary of offensive language and risky subject matter; while the use of four letter words and other eye-catching content may draw the reader's attention, it almost always has a negative impact because it raises questions about the candidate's judgment.

There are other areas where one ought to be mindful, but these will hopefully point you in the right direction for writing an essay that most appropriately reflects your skills.

Writing an Effective Essay

What can you do to write an effective essay?

- Write your essays ahead of time and revise them in later sittings.

- Write in a style that reflects your personality.

- Have a teacher, a family member, a counselor, and/or your peers proofread your essays.

- Write about topics that matter to you. Passion will usually bring out the best in your writing.

I always told students in my information sessions that the best essays come from the heart and not the head. Applicants who write about topics and issues that matter to them tend to write the most thoughtful, interesting, and passionate essays. Trying to force passion in an essay will come across as a contrived and inaccurate reflection of who the candidate is and what matters most to him or her. Some applicants try to present what they believe admissions officers want to read, but of course they don't know enough about the personalities and backgrounds of the readers. Simply stated, good essays are personal, they support what admissions offices most likely already know about the candidate, and they're written with a good sense of grammar and style.

Interviewing

The interview gives candidates an opportunity to market themselves and their strengths to those who may advocate or even determine their admission fate. For the admissions office, the interview can be a recruiting opportunity, a screening tool, or a public relations vehicle for the university.

Most of the highly selective universities offer some type of interview—with admissions officers or with individuals hired by the admissions office. Some universities also offer alumni interviews with a former student. I would encourage the applicant to take advantage of the opportunity to interview. A positive report, in which the interviewer is able to laud your personal appeal and strength of character, can be a valuable addition to any folder. If in fact an admissions office requests that you schedule an alumni interview, do not decline unless there are extenuating circumstances for refusing.

TIP: *Although schools mention that interviews are optional, turning down an invitation to interview may be interpreted as a lack of interest in the institution.*

Interviews are typically done on campus through the admissions office or regionally through extensive alumni networks interested in attracting and meeting with strong local candidates. On-campus interviews may carry slightly more weight because the interviewers are either part of the decision-making body or are well known by the decision makers, but on-campus interviews are not absolutely necessary.

Admissions offices understand that while many students schedule summer interviews while taking the pre-senior year college tour have the financial resources to visit and interview on a number of campuses, some of the most exceptional candidates either do not have the resources or the time to come to campus for an interview. This is why extensive national networks have been developed to offer candidates interviews with local alumni. The on-campus interview is not necessarily the best forum for all candidates either. A poor interview report from a seasoned admissions officer can fatally wound the candidacy of an otherwise strong case.

The interview also can provide a valuable perspective to the admissions committee by allowing an alumnus or an admissions officer or another member of the university to offer his or her impressions of a candidate. In trying to differentiate among the talented candidates in the applicant pool, admissions officers are looking for insight from people who understand the university and how the candidate might contribute to it. While Letters of Recommendation reveal a good deal about an applicant's personal qualities, nearly all of them are extremely positive, and the interview presents a first or close secondhand validation or repudiation of those qualities. And in addition to the more neutral perspective when an interview is conducted by someone who represents the university, the interview report offers still one more viewpoint on the candidate.

Interviews help create a clearer picture when determining the personal match between the candidate and the institution, but a top-flight interview report is not a necessity for admission. A sure-fire admission with glowing school reports, powerful academic credentials, and a clear extracurricular niche in the college will not be hindered by an average interview report. For example, a candidate to Harvard from Claremont, California, had a powerful transcript, with a 1540 SAT I result and three 800s on the SAT II tests. His extracurricular activities were solid too: editor in chief of the school newspaper, community service, and lots of lab research. The interview, however, was somewhat lukewarm from a personal charm perspective, but the interviewer acknowledged how talented the candidate was and gave a strong recommendation for admission. Ultimately, he was admitted to the class.

132

At the same time, a stellar interview report for a candidate with weak to modest credentials will most likely not elevate him or her to a level considered worthy of admission. I'd estimate that the interview has a marginal impact on 20 to 25 percent of the cases admitted. For these candidates, the quantitative credentials and highly specialized skills speak so clearly that a bland interview is of little real consequence. But while interviews do not make a tremendous impact on cases at the extremes, the interview report becomes a key component for the large segment of cases considered to be at the "edge" of admission.

By the "edge," I refer to highly qualified candidates whose credentials are excellent but not compelling within the applicant pool; these students therefore comprise the "choices" that an admissions committee must ultimately make. As the saying goes, the devil you know is better than the one you don't know, and admissions officers like to know what they're getting in an applicant. Generally speaking, universities are conservative and risk averse, and any selection committee is less willing to take risks on candidates they have less positive information on, particularly in personal terms. The interview can be a good way of revealing more about potential, personal appeal and "fit" with the college, and accordingly answer or raise any questions about what the candidate has to offer the campus.

The interview can also pose problems for some applicants, especially for excessively shy or anxious candidates. A perfectly strong case on paper can be weakened or exposed when a nervous or more introverted personality is revealed in the interview. Though a candidate does not need an effusive personality to have a quality interview, interviewers are searching for depth, and an exceedingly high level of reticence or shyness can make it difficult for an interviewer to find. For those who consider themselves weak at interviewing, the best advice I can give is to practice your communication skills by engaging adults in conversation whenever you can. The college interview may be the first interview that seemingly matters, but it's only the first step in a lifetime of interviewing for jobs, graduate schools, scholarships, grants, and other endeavors in which personal qualities mean something.

For those who choose to request or are required to interview as part of the application, it's important to understand what a good interviewer is trying to learn about you in the 30 to 60 minutes that you'll be with him or her. On the surface, many of the questions asked are meant to provide background information and detail about some of your experiences. How is senior year going for you? What classes are you taking, and have any of them been particularly challenging? How do you spend your time outside of the classroom? And you'll be asked to discuss one or two of the extracurricular activities that are most important to you. These are leading questions designed to open more engaging and interesting lines of conversation that will hopefully unveil some of your true passions and interests.

Both the interviewer and admissions officers are trying to glean as much information as they can about you, and a good interview report can delve deeper into some of the important questions that admissions officers seek to have answered about a candidate:

- What kind of interpersonal skills does the candidate possess?

- How might the candidate handle the challenges and demands of a highly selective institution?

- Does the candidate have potential, and is she or he living up to that potential?

- What kind of roommate will this person be? Would you or others want to room with this candidate?

- Is the candidate motivated or does he or she show initiative?

- What are the candidate's leading passions? Are they more intellectual, personal, or extracurricular in nature?

- What qualities about the candidate are the most or least impressive?

If you consider these questions from the admissions perspective, the interview is designed to provide a gauge with degrees of comparison. The interview can uncover strengths and possibly flaws in character, reveal passion for and depth within activities that may have been over-looked in the application, and offer insight and detail about the candidate that might have otherwise not been properly accentuated.

Intangibles: Tip Factors

Admissions offices refer to factors that can influence an individual's application as "tips," "tags," or "hooks." The principle behind this nomenclature is that admissions staffs are looking at a whole host of factors that might tip the balance in favor of a candidate based upon his or her talents, background, and experiences. We'll examine the intangible factors, or tips, in five categories:

- Geographic and School Diversity

- Socioeconomic and Ethnic Diversity

- Alumni, Faculty, and Special Interest Cases

- The Futures Test and Life After College

- Heartstrings Cases

We've already discussed the more tangible tip factors and tags placed upon applicants with specific academic and extracurricular talents. In addition to a "tip" that might be associated with a student who had a penchant for Classics or the virtuoso violinist, students may receive additional consideration based upon traits that would support the objective of enrolling a diverse student body. These traits alone will not be the determining factor in a candidate's application, but when these characteristics are tied together—be it background, career goals, or other interests—the personal factors can help sway the committee in the favor of a candidate.

Investigating the intangible factors, to discern in them a candidate's overall strengths and weaknesses, is a complex art. It involves an assessment of how these factors have influenced the individual, requiring an admissions committee to evaluate how important these factors have been in shaping the candidate, the impact these characteristics might have on campus, and the significance of these tags when considered in the larger admissions context.

On the individual level, admissions officers consider a candidate's experiences and background and how they might have impacted on one's opportunities for achievement. Personal and environmental factors such as geographic, socioeconomic, parental, ethnic, international, and religious background are among the tip factors that give committee members a better understanding of how candidates have made the most of the resources available to them. Although each of these factors have varying levels of significance for an individual candidate, in combination they're important in telling the student's story.

Compelling stories come in so many forms, it's somewhat unfair to try to characterize them in neat little buckets; however, it's useful to see how some of these more intangible factors can make a difference for some candidates. The story of a first-generation immigrant who has achieved a high level of success in a new country with a new language and culture can carry as much weight in the process as the suburban high-level, all-around strong candidate who has been a school leader. The small-town farming family applicant and the child of a blue-collar mechanic living in the heart of an urban center are viewed in a similarly positive manner. The international student who can bring a unique perspective and set of experiences to campus is no less appealing than the son or daughter of an alumnus who is applying for admission. While there are countless permutations of how these tips can shape an admissions case, let's look at three areas where the tip can have a prominent role: geographic diversity, socioeconomic and ethnic diversity, and alumni and special interest cases.

Geographic and School Diversity

Ivy League schools seek to attract the most talented students from all parts of the world, and enrolling a highly talented and geographically diverse student body requires successful recruiting efforts by admissions offices and alumni networks. The farther the distance between an applicant's home and the university campus, the more difficult it can be to attract and enroll the candidate. Consider, for instance, the lure of merit scholarship awards that highly competitive state university systems can offer certain students who might otherwise prefer schools farther from their homes.

Although highly selective schools have fared well in attracting students from different geographic backgrounds, a high percentage of those who enroll tend to live within the area or region. At Brown, 24 percent of the student body hails from New England and 29 percent from the Mid-Atlantic states, while 14 percent come from the Pacific states, 12 percent from the Southern states, and 13 percent from the Central, Mountain, and Midwest states.[3] Similarly at Harvard, 19 percent are from New England, 25 percent come from the Mid-Atlantic states, while the other regions trail behind at 18 percent each from both the Pacific and the South, and 12 percent from the Midwest.[4]

The states with the highest representation on campus fall, not surprisingly, into two categories: those states located near the university, and states with the largest populations. California rates among the top five states in terms of total admitted and enrolled students at nearly every Ivy school. In 2001, Penn matriculated more than 50 freshmen from California, Texas, Florida, Pennsylvania, New York, New Jersey, Massachusetts, Connecticut, and Maryland.[5] For states like California and New York, the numbers will push close to 200 admitted students across all of the Ivy League schools. At Stanford, 39.6 percent of the more than 2400 admitted students to the class of 2005 were from California, 8.4 percent from Texas, and 5.9 percent from New York.[6] Highly selective schools also enroll a large percentage of students who reside within its own state's borders. Cornell admits a huge number of students from New York State—nearly 40 percent of the entire undergraduate enrollment in 2001—and UPenn has a tremendous commitment to residents from Pennsylvania, and in particular from Philadelphia, where the school is located.

At the other end of the spectrum, highly selective schools spend a significant amount of time and money trying to recruit students from areas of the country where they have seen fewer applications. Admissions offices have dedicated resources to improve recruitment of qualified candidates from lesser populated states like Wyoming, the Dakotas, Montana, Alaska, and West Virginia. Residing in a college's "backyard" or living in a state that sends fewer applications will not be the defining factor in any case, but geography can be a tip in the candidate's favor. The son of a farming family from the Plains states, a rancher's child from Wyoming or the Southwest, or an applicant with a rural background from any region will be viewed positively in the geographic context.

Similarly, students who apply from urban settings where a selective school might not regularly see applicants can get a geographic boost: Las Vegas is a perfect example. It is among the fastest growing urban areas in the country, yet the Ivy League schools find it difficult to recruit and attract students from the area. One reason that recruiting in rapidly growing communities is difficult is the lack of quality education in school systems strapped by the demands of managing huge enrollments.

As the landscape of the country changes, school systems are an increasingly important connection between the geographic tip and the weight it is given for a candidate. A student attending a rural school with seven students in the senior class will not have the same opportunities available in other settings. Poorer communities, whether rural, urban, or suburban, with limited offerings to students will always receive a school or geographic bump, especially if there are fewer applicants from these areas.

The exception to the rule is a recent transplant to an area that might get a tip for geography. One of the first questions asked when a case is presented with a geographic "tip" is: How long has the candidate lived in the region? It's hard to make an area argument for an applicant from Taos, New Mexico, who moved there from a major city like Los Angeles only a year or two earlier. The underlying current in these discussions often revolves around students taking advantage of the resources available to them, and the growth opportunity for someone who becomes exposed to the wide array of possibilities that a highly selective education can provide.

In addition to a tip for poorer school systems, schools that send few applicants get a slight tip. New school districts or schools where the applications are few and far between raise the attention of readers. Admitting such a student helps build a presence in these areas and may attract other applicants from the area in the future. Seeing applications every year from Indianapolis schools like Carmel and Park Tudor is not uncommon, while coming across a viable application from Lawrence Central may pique a committee's interest, since its students do not send many applications to Harvard. Strong school systems that have established reputations also receive a boost when the selection process gets tight since a track record of past student successes brings with it a level of comfort to admissions offices.

The scope of international admissions has become increasingly important in college admissions in recent years. Attracting candidates from beyond the United States improves a university's position in the global community in academia, politics, and business. With global markets expanding and the political climate itself becoming globalized, graduates with a background and interest in international affairs, both from within the country and without, are in high demand. Thus, the nation's elite schools are aggressively seeking individuals who show promise in politics, finance, and business.

Over the last several years, Ivy League schools have seen a rapid rise in the number of international applications and admissions. In 2001 about 8 percent of the Cornell undergraduate student body and approximately 9 percent of Yale undergraduates came from international backgrounds, while about 9 percent of Brown's class of 2005 and 8 percent of the class of 2005 at Harvard were international students. Over the next decade these numbers will probably rise as more students abroad seek to take advantage of the world-renowned educations offered in America. Even during these uncertain times in international politics, many selective institutions have continued to expand their recruiting efforts to seek and to educate leaders from different parts of the world.

For nearly all the Ivy League schools and nearly all of the top U.S. institutions, Canada leads the way in international admissions. Singapore, the United Kingdom, India, and Pakistan also send large numbers of students to highly selective schools in the United States annually. It's not uncommon to have foreign students representing 70 to 100 countries at an Ivy League college. For many of these countries, the admission rate is far below that of the admission rate for students who apply from the United States.

A more subtle point in the rise of international admissions is its effect on domestic student applicants. Admissions offices are not looking to admit a set number of international candidates, but as the number of compelling international applications grows, the number of spaces offered to students from the United States is likely to decrease. In other words, the strong international pool will raise the bar for all applicants.

Socioeconomic and Ethnic Diversity

For years, diversity has been lauded as an indispensable aspect of what makes an Ivy League education so valuable. It helps create a stimulating educational environment for students, fostering a dynamic and vibrant community in which students have a unique opportunity to learn from one another.

Creating a diverse community requires not the admission of students from a variety of backgrounds and experiences, but that a sufficient number of students with similar experiences are admitted in order that they have a positive impact on campus. One student from Montana or a single hockey player from Alberta will make far less impact on a campus than a group of students from Montana or a team of hockey players from all over the world. From an admissions perspective, in order to "provide a truly heterogeneous environment that reflects the rich diversity of the United States, [diversity] cannot be provided without some attention to the numbers."[7]

Following the 1978 Supreme Court ruling in *University of California v. Bakke,* a more narrowly tailored definition of diversity evolved on campuses in the 1980s and 1990s. *Ethnic* diversity was emphasized. While I value its importance in the college environment, in my opinion the media and legal attention that has been given to the role of ethnic diversity in admissions has obscured the true benefits that a diverse educational environment creates. It's the connection between ethnic and socioeconomic factors as the demographics rapidly shift in America during the first decade of the new century that need real attention within our nation's highly selective admissions offices. To me, socioeconomic and ethnic diversity are two of the most important tips in the admissions process, and too often these areas are discussed independent of one another.

Having grown up as a lower-middle-class kid who lived in Boston and Quincy, Massachusetts, I view myself as somewhat of an outsider to the Ivy League world. Neither of my parents went to college, and I had no idea about the true value of a Harvard education, but my parents taught me to value what a good education could provide. While we may have perceived the path of an Ivy education more in terms of leading to a financially secure, upwardly mobile employment track, what I learned from my peers—who came from many countries, with many religious, socioeconomic, and ethnic backgrounds—was more than could be defined by dollars and cents. As the costs of higher education rise, and as the income gap in America increases, highly selective admissions offices need to maintain a commitment to educating and training outstanding students from all economic walks of life.

Most Ivy League schools aggressively compete for students who have shown true promise, regardless of economic circumstances, by asking how the candidate has made the most of the resources available to him or her. In addition to the recruitment of distinguished candidates from modest backgrounds, highly selective schools have also taken on the task of making an Ivy education affordable to all students who are admitted. This kind of commitment has made an incredible impact on thousands of modest to poor students who have had the opportunity to fulfill the American educational dream.

This is particularly significant now, at a time of increasing economic inequality in the United States. As far back as 1992, scholars like Mickey Kaus spoke of the growing income gap between the poorer and upper-middle-class in America. During the unprecedented economic boom of the 1990s, the middle-class family has all but vanished and been replaced with what many have termed as an economic "underclass."[8] According to the U.S. Bureau of Labor Statistics, graduating high school student populations will continue to rise, from 2.8 million in 2000 to 3.2 million by 2008. Not surprisingly, the most significant shifts within population demographics are connected to socioeconomic and ethnic changes that the country will experience in the next six to ten years. There will be significant increases in the percentages of Hispanic, Asian, and African American populations in high school graduating classes, and census projections estimate a significant percentage jump in Asian and Hispanic populations with a proportionate percentage decline in white non-Latino populations. With a rapidly changing population and intense legal scrutiny on admissions policies, examining ethnic diversity in a vacuum is the slippery slope in the admissions world today.

Since the *Bakke* decision, many state university systems have attempted to defend formulaic admissions processes when it comes to minority students. The legal challenges that have been settled at the state and circuit court levels within state university systems in Texas and Georgia, and the present state of affairs of minority admissions in Michigan, has changed the landscape of minority admissions across the country. Critics of *Bakke* and the role of ethnic diversity in admissions point to poorly planned and conceived admissions processes in the state universities in the wake of the decision, and they advocate for a strict academic meritocracy in college admissions.

University leaders and politicians must measure the risks of an academic meritocracy based on standardized exams and be wary of the inflexibility that such a process might place on highly selective institutions. Implementing a system that shifts the process away from one of its strengths—which is its ability to admit students whose special traits may not be identified through a series of standardized examinations—could have a significant impact on the kinds of students who attend highly selective schools in the future.

At the moment, the highly selective private universities have been able to maintain their commitment to admitting candidates from underrepresented minority backgrounds. For the classes of 2005, over 34 percent of those admitted to Dartmouth were students of color, as were 37 percent of those admitted to Princeton and more than 49 percent admitted to Stanford.[9] But though these numbers are significant, the number of students who actually attend these schools is far lower since many have also been admitted by other highly competitive universities. In 2001, for example, about 27 percent of Princeton's and 45 percent of Stanford's student bodies come from minority backgrounds, according to the schools, and both numbers are lower than the admissions rates listed above.

In terms of minority recruiting and admissions, African American, Asian American, Hispanic, and Native American (including Pacific Islander and Native Hawaiian) students receive a tip that is evaluated in the context of the entire application. As U.S. Census changes introduce more broad ethnic designations, more applicants are choosing to identify themselves as multiethnic or biracial in the application.

The degree that a tip for minority status has is based on a number of factors. For example, it may have more meaning for the candidate who has been engaged with and committed to his or her culture in some way for an extended period of time. Geography, family history, and socioeconomic status will also boost the candidate's competitiveness. By talking together about their experiences and values, a Native Alaskan born and raised on Kodiak Island, an immigrant Cambodian American adjusting to the culture of American urban life, a Mexican American who excels in the harsh economic environment of East Los Angeles, or an African American who has succeeded in the rural deep South can offer much to their peers.

The depth of quality candidates within minority cross sections also determines the degree of the tip an applicant might receive. Asian Americans represent the largest percentage of the minority applicant and admitted student pool, and this may lessen the importance of a tip based on ethnic background alone. But students from underrepresented cultures within the Asian American community may still receive a significant edge. For example, applicants from Cambodian, Thai, and Vietnamese American backgrounds tend to be less numerous than Indian, Chinese, or Taiwanese American applicants.

For some of the most underrepresented minority groups, there are correspondingly fewer strong applications that make their way to admissions committee meetings. Ivy League schools recruit heavily to identify and attract applications from highly qualified African American, Mexican American, Native American, and Puerto Rican students, for instance, because there are fewer strong candidates from these backgrounds. Admissions offices make every effort to tip the scales, should all things be equal between these applicants and others. Highly selective schools end up competing against one another for these candidates.

Admissions offices also make significant attempts to admit students from the large minority population bases that are rapidly growing and changing the shape of the demographics within the United States. Although the numbers might vary from school to school, admissions rates for students from African American, Mexican American, and Puerto Rican applicants at the most highly selective schools tend to be higher than the admissions rates for (non-Mexican, non-Puerto Rican) Hispanic American, Asian American, and white applicants. In addition to responding to the country's changing demographics, the slightly higher admissions rate for these minority students reflects recruiting efforts which have seen universities spend more resources, financial and otherwise, identifying and seeking candidates who will be strong contenders for admission earlier in the process. Highly selective schools have started building relationships with applicants earlier in high school, helping to advise students on what preparation is needed to become strong candidates for admission.

There are also some very good independent organizations, such as Prep for Prep and A Better Chance, that begin the process of preparing minority students from disadvantaged backgrounds for a university education in middle school and high school. Highly selective schools have sought to build relationships with these programs as well. These programs help place minority students into private, parochial, and public exam high schools, and they mentor and give support to students who might not otherwise be encouraged or able to prepare for a rigorous high school education.

Of course, regardless of one's socioeconomic and ethnic background, the sum of the parts has to come together in the application. The candidate will rise or fall on academic, extracurricular, and personal qualities as they relate to his or her chance of achieving success at the most highly selective schools.

Alumni, Faculty, and Special Interest Cases

Part of doing business in any environment is understanding who pays the bills. Giving additional consideration to children of alumni, faculty members, or other institutionally important cases is not a new phenomenon, nor is this type of tip isolated to only a handful of schools. School lineage has been a consideration in hundreds of private schools' admissions practices for years. Many schools depend on the philanthropy of successful alumni for expansion programs, development of infrastructure, and other financial assistance needed for providing a world-class education. Without such support, many of the resources and facilities available at our research universities today would not exist. In addition, outstanding achievements of faculty members and alumni build the prestige and reputation of these institutions.

Understanding the value of these relationships, admissions offices offer a tip to what would be characterized as special interest cases. The tip given to alumni children is generally only given to children whose parent(s) graduated from the undergraduate institution at the highly selective schools. Parents who attended one of the graduate schools or grandparents who attended the undergraduate institution do not typically receive the benefit of an additional tip for their offspring. There are variations in how the alumni tip is meted, so you may want to inquire at the specific schools to which you're considering submitting an application.

Similar to the other tips, the importance of the alumni tip is relative to the context of the entire application. Children of alumni are not admitted simply because their parents have attended the school; they must also present excellent academic and personal credentials as well. Admissions and development offices, however, are watchful of their alumni admissions rates. According to the class of 2005 profile, 40.8 percent of the children of alumni from the University of Pennsylvania who chose to apply to UPenn were admitted to the class. The total number of alumni children admitted to UPenn for the class of 2005 was 419 out of a total 3951 admissions.[10] While there is no percentage of spaces reserved for alumni children, it is reasonable to estimate that 5 to 15 percent of the admissions offers made each year are to legacy cases.

The high frequency of alumni children gaining admission each year is not solely due to the alumni tip factor. A significant majority of these students have impeccable credentials. It makes sense that alumni parents who experienced the challenges, expectations, and demands involved in aspiring to an education at a highly selective university involved themselves in their children's college preparation. Many children from successful Ivy League parents have been the beneficiaries of exceptional resources and fine educations that allowed them to develop their talents. Others may simply have the natural intellectual gifts necessary to be outstanding candidates in their own right.

As a whole, students from alumni backgrounds are every bit as appealing as others within the applicant pool. Each year there will be a handful, maybe as many as a half-dozen, alumni cases that are only reasonably qualified, but the alumni tip is particularly strong. The applicant may be less distinguished academically or in extracurricular activities, but almost without fail, these candidates have desirable personal appeal. In these cases, it makes perfect sense to give a boost to the candidate whose parents have been particularly loyal alumni.

Two other special interest cases are worthy of note.

Children of faculty receive additional consideration at all colleges. The significance of the tip ranges tremendously from automatic admission at some of the less competitive schools to careful review by an admissions or faculty committee. The tip can also be limited to certain faculties within the university or to certain teaching positions. At Harvard, with more than 11 faculties and a variety of teaching positions, the faculty tip was extended fully to all tenured faculty members of the College. The children of assistant and nontenured professors also were given strong consideration, and while children of other university faculty (Harvard Law School, Harvard Business School, etc.) were given careful review, these cases did not necessarily receive the same tip.

The second special interest case, development cases, involves students whose families have drawn an interest from the fundraising arm of the university. The most selective universities in the country are also among the most successful at raising money through a variety of capital campaigns. The development offices are keenly aware of the interest that some donors have in their children's or grandchildren's education, and each year they apprise admissions offices of those cases that are most important to the financial future of the institution.

While an admissions office will take notice when the development office has tagged a case, the most important element involved with evaluating a development case is to handle it with sensitivity. At the most competitive colleges, the majority of such cases will not be admitted without the corresponding academic credentials that would make them strong contenders within the applicant pool. Similar to the alumni and faculty tip, only a handful of places are offered each year to students who really need that tip to gain admission. Most of the cases that do have these tugs are solid if not exceptional candidates; the tip simply solidifies their space in the class.

Some have criticized the importance of athletics and minority recruiting, questioning whether some of these candidates are "deserving" enough based purely on their academic credentials. Others believe that the alumni tip is an unnecessary advantage given to candidates because it has nothing to do with an individual's talents. While being a legacy, a development case, a minority case, or a star pitcher can "heal the sick," these tips alone can't raise the dead. Applicants who won't find academic success at highly selective schools are not going to be admitted. There's too much competition to get into Ivy League schools to admit candidates who will flounder academically and socially, regardless of the strength of the candidate's tip. In fact, when all is said and done, only about 1 percent of candidates are admitted primarily because of a tip. And with graduation rates well over 90 percent, Ivy League schools may continue to have confidence that their policies regarding these tips are thoughtfully and fairly carried out.

The Futures Test and Life After College

As an admissions case is read, a story about the candidate begins to unfold. There is a story behind every applicant, and it is in the hands of the admissions office to measure how one's past experiences might shape the individual's future direction.

The "futures test, " as it's called, serves two purposes. An admissions office can look at an applicant's past experiences as a measure of the potential for meaningful contributions to his or her college and future endeavors. From an institutional perspective, projecting the path of an applicant based upon past achievements can also help admissions committees meet the college's objectives in the academic and professional world. Admissions offices are cognizant of the goals of the university and its student body, and it's with great care that admissions staffs delve into whether students will continue in the directions they indicate in their applications.

Of course, admissions professionals are not experts at predicting the future, and there are many students who take career or academic paths in college and after they have graduated that could not have been predicted. Admissions committees play the percentages, however, when reviewing candidates who might ultimately apply their talents in academia, service, politics, or whatever areas of life which they indicate in the application.

It's interesting to see how an admitted class and their many interests evolve over a four-year period. At Harvard, for example, the class of 2001 had a wide range of academic and extracurricular interests. Over 27 percent of the admitted students were interested in studying the biological sciences, approximately 25 percent were

151

in the humanities, 20 percent in the social sciences, 9 percent the physical sciences, 8 percent in engineering, 6 percent math, 3 percent computer science, and about 1 percent were undecided.[11] Students had a wide range of primary extracurricular interests too. More than 30 percent indicated that music would be one of their primary activities, 20 percent listed the arts, 19 percent public service, 17 percent journalism, 13 percent student government, and 9 percent debate. At the same time, more than 60 percent indicated an interest in some level of college athletics.[12]

This broad balance in the makeup of a class not only meets the diverse needs of a faculty that offers 30 or more majors to choose from, but it is also a solid basis for predicting the direction of the student body upon graduation. In fact, the graduation report often mirrors this range as graduates move into their professional careers or graduate school.

At the nation's highly selective schools, there is a healthy balance between attending graduate school and entering the workforce. As the strength of the economy shifts, so too will the number of graduates who enter the workforce, but the number of highly selective graduates who plan to obtain an advanced degree is astounding. In a given year, 16 to 20 percent of Harvard College graduates indicate an interest in attending medical school, about 12 to 15 percent express a desire to attend law school, about 6 to 8 percent plan to attend a master's or doctoral program, and 50 to 60 percent of the graduates plan on working upon graduation. And of those who choose to work, a significant number will head back to business school or continue their education at some other graduate institution later in life.

The future paths of graduates and alumni confirm the choices that an admissions office will make. Graduates who return to their home state to practice family medicine, earn their law degree and become attorneys, or become involved in local or national politics will make a significant impact on society and further validate the judicious decisions made during the admissions process.

Heartstrings Cases

Heartstrings cases are some of the most difficult to evaluate. These are cases in which the candidate has had to overcome tremendous adversity in some form. While admissions offices at highly selective schools consider objective criteria very carefully, subjective information—such as the personal challenges an applicant has had to face—do not go unnoticed. Many adolescents are faced with personal hardships that have a significant impact on their growth and personality. These might include dealing with the painful loss of a loved one, battling with serious personal health problems, handling their parents' divorce, or managing to thrive in a harsh or deprived environment. Whatever the situation or circumstance, the magnitude of adversity in some applicants' lives can be seen in their admissions folders.

One example of a case that tugged on our committee's heartstring, from the Denver, Colorado area, involved a Cambodian immigrant who had come to the United States at a young age. This applicant was Mr. Everything in his poor, urban public high school, and he had strong grades with SAT I scores in the low 1300 range. What was especially compelling in his case was the fact that he lived in a one-room apartment with seven members of his family. Can you imagine the obstacles he faced in trying to maintain strong grades in high school with such a family dynamic, a nearly full-time job, and responsibilities for caring for his younger siblings?

Another instance of achievement in the face of adversity concerned an applicant with SAT I scores in the 1500 range and a very solid extracurricular profile, despite the fact the she had been battling leukemia. Her high school was behind her like few others that year, and the admissions committee wrestled with offering a space to a candidate who would likely die before finishing college. After much discussion, she was admitted. She attended Harvard for two years before withdrawing and succumbing to leukemia.

Area or regional admissions officers who get to know the tangible and intangible depth of some of these cases become the strongest advocates for these candidates during committee meetings. These cases are strong from a quantitative perspective, but they're not necessarily "sure admits." The personal challenges these candidates face and the manner in which they've overcome the adversity appeal to the human element in the admissions process and to the sensitivities of the committee members. What makes these candidates even more compelling is their reluctance to draw attention to themselves or their adverse circumstances. From reading thousands of applications each year, I often found that those who faced the greatest challenges in life took little satisfaction in discussing these obstacles in a forum as "public" as a college application. Some may have written an essay about the impact of their difficulties, but more often it's the teacher letters, the interview report, or the counselor who enlightens the committee about the challenges an applicant has faced.

Another student, whose case has received national acclaim, moved from Oregon to the South Shore of Boston in middle school and lived in and out of a homeless shelter with her single mother for portions of her early high school years. Eventually she settled in with a foster family and began to perform exceptionally well in the classroom, while becoming a successful high school wrestler. Her writing and grades were impressive, and her essay outlined the dangers of living on the streets and in shelters as she depicted the horror of staying awake in her room while hearing the hallway violence. Her high school counselors pushed hard for her, and her interviews helped push her case over the top.

A final example of how candidates can make the most of the hand dealt to them came from the Buffalo, New York area. The candidate had learned to deal with adversity as a young child when he was diagnosed with a form of cancer that required the amputation of one leg below his knee. While his grades were strong, his SAT I scores were more modest, in the high 1300 to low 1400 range. What blew the committee away during admissions meetings was his character and commitment to giving back to others. The committee was also impressed with how he was able to turn his adversity as a child into such a motivating and positive factor. His school's support was extraordinary, and it was clear that there was something truly special about this young man. In addition to the personal testament on his behalf, he had also developed into a strong athlete as an ice hockey goaltender. Ultimately, he was admitted to Harvard and made a tremendous impact on the campus. Although not a recruited Division I athlete, he was a "walk-on" to the varsity team and became the first amputee ever to play Division I college ice hockey.

While these candidates offer only a few examples of how personal experiences can have a positive bearing on the outcome of an admissions case, not all of the cases that win the hearts of admissions officers will be able to be offered a space in their college. Many of these candidates become the ultimate "choices" in the process. They're the kinds of people who are loved on campus, but with such stiff competition, only some of the most compelling and accomplished are offered a space in the class.

Endnotes

1. University of Chicago Undergraduate Office of Admissions Application, 2002–2003, Essay Option 3.
2. *Harvard Crimson* staff, *50 Successful Harvard Application Essays* (New York: St Martin's Griffin, 1999).
3. Geographic Distribution of Matriculating Students, Fall 2001, Brown Web site, www.brown.edu/administration/admission/profile.html#geographic.
4. *Harvard Undergraduate Admissions 2000–2001 Viewbook and Application*, p. 26.
5. Geographic Distribution of the Class of 2005, UPenn Web site, www.upenn.edu/undergrad/applying/profile.html.
6. "Stanford Offers Admission to 2416 for the Class of 2005," *The Stanford Report*, April 4, 2001.
7. *University of California Regents v. Bakke,* 1978. Appendix to the Brief of Columbia University, Harvard University, Stanford University, and the University of Pennsylvania, as Amici Curiae, p. 52.
8. Mickey Kaus: *The End of Equality* (New York: Basic Books, 1992).
9. "Admissions Mails Letters to '05s Today," *The Dartmouth Online,* April 4, 2001. "1675 offered spots in Class of 2005," *Princeton Weekly Bulletin,* April 16, 2001: Vol. 90, No. 24. "Stanford Offers Admission to 2416 for the Class of 2005," *Stanford Report,* April 4, 2001.
10. University of Pennsylvania Class of 2005 Student Profile, www.upenn.edu/admissions/undergrad/applying/profile.php.
11. *Harvard University Gazette,* April 1, 1997.
12. Ibid.

PART II

COLLEGE ADMISSIONS 102: UNDERSTANDING THE ADMISSIONS CYCLE

RATING CANDIDATES AND THE EVALUATION PROCESS

Reading and Rating Your Application

Now that we've examined the areas of focus within admissions—academics, extracurricular activities, personal qualities, and the importance of "tips"—we can turn to the admissions process: how the application is read, evaluated, and presented during committee meetings.

For the majority of applications, only one or two readers will review the application folder. The first readers have the laborious task of transcribing all of a candidate's information onto a summary page that has a list of extracurricular and academic interests for the reader to highlight or circle. The demographic, personal, school, and parental data from the application itself is also included on this sheet. There's also space for each reader to enter ratings and comments about the candidate. Given the amount of information that must be transcribed, a strong application can take as long as 40 minutes to read and evaluate in its initial reading.

The first reader is also responsible for determining whether an application should be passed on to a second reader for review. At some schools, all applications are evaluated by a primary and a secondary reader as a way of validating initial impressions, but other schools rely on experienced readers to filter cases down to contending candidates for the second reader's analysis. At Harvard, for example, not every application will be read by multiple readers, but the high-level credentials will be presented during large committee meetings. The less experienced readers will pass more cases on for a second review, for quality assurance, than more seasoned readers. In my first year of reading, I passed about 70 percent of all the applications I read to a second reader, but later, in my second and third years of admissions, I probably sent only 30 to 40 percent on for a second reading.

Admissions offices have developed their own methodologies for assessing quantitative and qualitative ratings and adding comments to an application. The rating system and written comments are important because the application must be summarized in an accessible format that can be used to compare all candidates. It also allows admissions officers who did not read a particular application to review its highlights during committee meetings in order to compare it with applications that he or she did read. The admissions office can therefore create a standard that will be applicable "coast to coast" and worldwide. And with the uniform standards candidate ratings present, more staff members can participate in decision-making meetings and assess certain areas of the application.

Most admissions offices require numerical ratings for the overall assessment, academics, extracurricular activities, and personal qualities. Teacher recommendations and the secondary school report typically receive ratings to measure the level of support from the high school. If an admissions office offers alumni or on-campus interviews, there may be a rating included with the written summary about the applicant. At many colleges, including those in the Ivy League, candidates who are recruited to play a varsity sport are also given an athletic rating.

Each highly selective school has its own scale for rating candidates, so the numerical ratings are less important for our purposes than understanding the range and purpose of the ratings in order to get a better feel for how you will compare to your peers in a particular area. Understanding the rating system might also give you a better perspective on where you stand in comparison to others in the applicant pool. In order to simplify the complexity of the different schools' rating systems, the comments—or "prose," in admissions committee vernacular—corresponds with the four general categories that most schools use to assess candidates. For our purposes, I have used prose that corresponds to Harvard's numerical rating system in each of the areas where ratings are required.

Academic Rating

The academic rating uses objective and qualitative data in concert with Letters of Recommendation, faculty review, or other sources—such as summer school transcripts—to evaluate candidates in the academic realm.

> *Potential Summa degree candidate.* Top grades, high standardized scores (above 750 in SAT I and SAT II, numerous AP scores of 5 or IB scores of 7), strong support letters,

possible outstanding faculty read, and/or recipient of nationally recognized academic awards.

Potential Magna/Honors degree candidate. Strong academic record (top 5 percent of class), good test scores (low to mid-700s, with more AP scores of 5 than 4 or IB scores of 6 or 7), strong support letters. Faculty read and other awards will be less compelling than those given the highest academic rating.

Solid candidate, possible Honors degree. Good grades (top 10 to 15 percent of class), solid test scores (mid-600s to low 700s, mix of passing AP or IB scores), support letters warm but do not place academic ability in "best in years" category.

Fair to marginal academic candidate. Decent grades, modest test scores (low 600s and below, average AP scores or no scores to report).

Applicants rated in the fair to marginal academic range will need to be unusually strong in other areas, including personal qualities, to have any chance at admission. Candidates in this category have about a 5 to 7 percent chance for admission, at best.

Extracurricular Rating

This rating does not typically include athletics, since varsity athletic recruits need to be flagged for review, for both Academic Index assessment and Ivy League reporting. For our purposes, however, I have included athletic ratings under this extracurricular listing.

National talent. Unusual strength in one or more areas, a potential major contributor on campus. National recognition for activity—varsity athletic recruit, national caliber musician, national entertainment experience (movies, theater, television), etc.

Strong local and/or secondary school contributor. Leader within school or community. Possible state level recognition for talent. Multisport captain with strong interest in college athletics—not a varsity recruited athlete.

Solid contributor. Involved in school or local activities but lacking in distinction, achievement, or leadership. High school varsity athlete.

Little or no contributions to activities or athletics.

Candidates who have physical conditions, family circumstances, or work responsibilities that prohibit them from becoming engaged in EC or athletic pursuits will be noted with a special rating and not be penalized.

Personal Rating

The personal rating draws from Letters of Recommendation, interviews, essays, and other facets of the application that help provide a snapshot of the candidate.

Rare personal appeal. "Best in career" candidate, extraordinary praise according to support and interview(s).

Standout. Candidate possesses excellent intrapersonal skills. "Best in years" praise according to support and interview.

Outstanding. Strong personal appeal and within the top tier in the year's applicant pool according to support and interview(s).

Positive. Nice person, positive support. Impressions based on support and interviews are good but not distinctive (more neutral in tone).

Questionable to poor. Recommendations are lukewarm to negative. Interview does not recommend candidate. Questions exist about his or her character or integrity.

Overall Rating

This overall recommendation on the admission status of the candidate takes into account all of the other ratings.

Clear admit. Quantitative and qualitative credentials place the candidate in the top 1 to 5 percent of the admission pool. Chances for admission: 95 percent or better.

Strong contender. Excellent credentials across the board with national caliber accomplishments in a number of areas. Chances for admission: 50 to 75 percent.

Good candidate. Above average credentials, though the candidate may be lacking national distinction. Chances for admission: 20 to 40 percent.

Marginal to poor candidate. Credentials are reasonable but generally below others in the applicant pool. Chances for admission: less than 5 percent.

The overall ranking is the best measurement for determining the likelihood of a candidate gaining admission. In order for an applicant who received an overall ranking of "clear admit" not to be offered a space, important information that had been previously missing from the application would have to surface. These might

164

include integrity issues, such as falsifying the application, incurring problems with the law, or being disciplined or suspended from school; having a marked academic decline; or receiving an abominable yet well-supported interview report. I've seen each of these occur during an admissions cycle.

Nearly all of the candidates admitted to highly selective universities will be rated in the top two categories in at least two of the areas discussed, excluding the school support ratings. The school support for almost every applicant has at least one "very strong" or higher rating.

The most common profile of an admitted student generally has an overall rating of "strong contender," with two other category ratings (among academic, extracurricular, and personal) in the same range or higher. We refer to this type of candidate as a "high-level all-arounder."

Candidates who receive the highest overall rating, "clear admit," are much less common. They represent the top 1 percent of the applicant pool and have some truly amazing gifts and accomplishments to support their case. To receive an overall rating of "clear admit," the applicant probably has been rated at this level in at least one other area.

Another common profile is the specialized applicant who is a star in one area but is more "standard strong" in others. Receiving a "clear admit" in the academic, extracurricular/athletic, or personal qualities ratings puts the applicant in a good position but does not ensure admission. To solidify one's place in the class, this applicant will most likely need to receive "strong contender" level support and have strong personal qualities. Applicants who may have a "good candidate" rating will need significantly higher ratings in the other areas, and perhaps will need compelling tips that may sway the balance of votes in their favor.

School Support and Teacher Recommendations

The teacher Letters of Recommendation and the counselor reports are usually the only letters that receive a rating. Supplementary recommendations and letters submitted by nonacademic subject teachers may be noted or written about in the reader sheet but will most likely not receive a numeric rating.

> *Unusually strong support.* "Best in career," "best in years" prose that offers detailed and specific examples.

> *Very strong support.* "One of the best this year" in-depth supporting prose.

> *Positive support.* Prose may lack superlatives, but the impressions of the candidate are very favorable.

> *Modest to negative support.* Teachers or school explicitly comment on the poor fit between the candidate and the institution. In some cases there may be a more implicit "muted" prose that catches the reader's attention. In other instances calls are made to admissions offices in order to avoid putting less than positive comments on paper.

Who Reads Your Application?

Even with a comprehensive rating system that quantifies talents and strengths, there is still a prominent "human element" in the process. During committee meetings, staff members discuss cases, compare applicants from across the country, and make many choices from the applicant pool that will help shape class dynamics. The profiles for the clear admits are so compelling that conversations are short and the decision is easy. For the large majority of cases, however, the committee meetings help to compare candidates' strengths from "coast to coast" and around the globe.

Those who make the fine distinctions and choices in selecting the class must have a thoughtful approach to the human aspects of selecting applicants, excellent reading and listening skills, a sense of humor, and patience. In addition, the most successful admissions offices consist of people who have a strong knowledge of the undergraduate experience, past and present.

The choices that committees make are subjective decisions based on objective criteria. However, there's a significant flexibility in the process, with admissions officers advocating for cases they believe are special. It was this human element that made the process compelling for me. I could see I could make a difference in some students' lives by advocating their cases. The level of input that individual admissions committee members have will vary from school to school, but their professional and personal imprints are left on the summary sheets through the entire committee process. Most offices place the decision-making responsibility in the hands of committees that make recommendations to a larger body, in the presence of the dean and possibly faculty members. At Harvard, a majority vote of the approximately 35 members of the admissions committee is required for admission.

As faculty and admissions officers examine the range of experiences and talents that applicants bring to the table, there is always room for individual value judgments about which factors are the most appealing and compelling. Some admissions officers may believe that a noncollege background is a particularly compelling tip, others may have an affinity for classical musicians, and still others may have a penchant for small-town applicants. The people who read the applications balance their professional expertise with these personal preferences and offer their perspective to the committee. Based on my interactions with other highly selective admissions staffs, I find that deans of admission work hard to build a diverse staff that brings a variety of viewpoints and backgrounds to the office.

Just as an admissions office is responsible for building a class each year, it also needs to build a team of staff members who will be able to recruit, admit, and matriculate the highest caliber of students possible. Ivy League colleges have worked hard to dispel the perception that their admissions offices are composed of old tweed-coated curmudgeons who have made a career of the profession and are out of touch with the present-day student body. Most college admissions offices today have found success in employing a balance between experienced officers, who understand the nuances of the process and institutional goals of the university, and younger, less experienced staff members who bring a fresh perspective to the table as recent college graduates. In many cases the recent graduates attended the schools where they work and are valuable as recruiting vehicles because they can speak from recent firsthand knowledge about their alma mater to prospective students. Turnover among the younger staff can be significant, since there are few senior positions available for newer staff members to move into, which may explain why there are fewer mid-career admissions officers in many Ivy League offices.

In a widely talented, experienced, and diverse admissions staff, each officer's strengths will be highlighted so others can learn from his or her experience. A truly interesting and impressive mix of people worked on the Harvard admissions staff, and our office regularly turned to specific committee members who had backgrounds in music, art, or athletics for more input about a candidate. Although there are fluctuations in the makeup of a staff from year to year due to turnover, to give you a sense of how valuable having a dynamic staff can be in the process of building a class, I'll provide a sample snapshot of the staff at Harvard from one particular year.

Approximately 30 members of the staff read applications and are part of the admissions committee each year. In the sample year I'll draw upon, about one-third of the committee had fewer than 5 years of admissions experience, another third had up to 15 years' experience, and the remaining third of the staff have had more. Slightly more than half of the staff were female, and nearly one-third of the staff members represented a range of minority backgrounds. About half of the sample admissions officers had Harvard undergraduate degrees, and the office made an active effort to recruit young Harvard alumni to the staff. Other admissions officers attended a range of schools, including selective institutions such as Yale, Princeton, the University of Virginia, and Colgate. Nearly all staff members had a degree in liberal arts, while a number also had a master's degree and several others had terminal degrees such as a Ph.D., a J.D., or an MBA.

Geographically, staff members came from many states, including Arkansas, Delaware, Florida, Kentucky, Illinois, Maine, Massachusetts, Minnesota, Missouri, Nebraska, New York, Ohio, Pennsylvania, Tennessee, and Virginia. They had attended public, private, and parochial institutions from a variety of school system sizes and settings. Several admissions officers entered the admissions world with other professional experience in engineering, journalism, the arts, education, or teaching. The extracurricular interests of the staff included music and performing arts, fine arts, and/or athletics in college. Some had deeply explored interests in musical performance, such as one staff member who played the double bass and another who played the piano. Many engaged the university community heavily, and others, including myself, had played a varsity sport at Harvard. This broad range of experience and interests ensured that committee discussions were lively, thoughtful, and thorough as the group attempted to admit a well-rounded class.

Keep in mind that officers at most selective schools are usually assigned regions of the country or specific schools for which they become the primary admissions representative. Others may read or review the application, but there will be one person with the primary responsibility of understanding their regions' schools in detail. These officers read all applications from those regions, communicate with candidates and the schools when necessary, and present the merits of each case to the committee.

Fall Recruiting

It's important to understand the admissions cycle and how the cycle interacts with individual applicants. Each fall, for starters, admissions officers hit the pavements to visit thousands of schools and to tout the benefits of the institutions they represent. At most of the highly selective schools, admissions representatives spend four to ten weeks each year traveling and recruiting.

The goal of fall recruiting is to build the "brand" recognition of the university and to encourage strong candidates to apply. Fall recruiting is also the last push for many schools to encourage candidates to consider applying to an early admissions program. With more and more talented students trying to determine the "right school" to apply to during their senior year, the importance of a strong fall recruiting program that can direct them to a particular university early admission program can't be underestimated.

Recruiting strategies abound, and university admissions offices market themselves to students in a number of ways. They attend college fairs, visit high schools, conduct evening programs, and utilize extensive mailing campaigns to identify and recruit candidates who may be interested in their institutions. National universities rely on their extensive alumni network to identify strong local candidates, and, aside from potential athletic recruits, alumni are urged to encourage top students to consider their alma maters.

Direct marketing is another way in which colleges reach out to prospective candidates. Universities, most often in the spring or summer of junior year, begin mailing brochures to highlight the features and benefits of their institution over their competitors. While some students may contact a university first with an inquiry, most students' names are purchased from the College Board, which, based upon test scores and other demographic data, sells high school students' names for recruiting purposes. It is an expensive but effective way for universities to target candidates based upon SAT tests, academic interests, and ethnicity, among other selection criteria. Some schools are even looking into e-mail as a source of recruiting.

One of the more cost-effective ways admissions offices have found for reaching a large audience of qualified candidates is through collaborative recruiting efforts with other selective institutions. For a number of years, Duke, Georgetown, Harvard, and Penn have traveled together in a joint effort to attract a larger audience of candidates from a wider geographic region who might be interested in learning about a number of colleges at one event. This year, the joint travel program will visit 110 cities. Cornell, Dartmouth, Tufts, and Yale have also traveled together recently. These joint programs also decrease the expense each one of the schools might incur if it were to conduct such a program on its own.

There are also some real advantages in conducting programs with other selective schools that have clear differences in their academic offerings. While it might make sense for Harvard, Princeton, and Yale to conduct joint programs together, for example, the differences between them are subtle and much more difficult to discern than schools that have significant geographic differences, diverse school histories, and distinct academic programs. Such diversely matched programs have been successful recruiting ventures for admissions offices.

Recruiting programs with a particular focus, such as a regional minority program or an initiative designed to recruit women interested in science, can successfully attract candidates in areas of particular interest to the university. With targeted programs, admissions offices can utilize the specialized talents or interests of admissions staff, students, or faculty to speak with students in person. These programs are among the most effective means for attracting talented candidates from specific areas or backgrounds. Even with larger regional and targeted marketing efforts, admissions representatives try to make as much personal contact with prospective candidates as possible. Whenever one is working in a larger setting, however, it can be difficult to record and remember the candidate for follow-up purposes. In the best-case scenarios, admissions follow-up will occur through letters, or possibly phone calls, from current undergraduates.

Visiting High Schools

The best and most personal way for admissions officers to meet and attract top candidates is through the traditional method of visiting high schools to speak with small groups of interested students. Late each summer and early fall, admissions offices arrange to meet and interact with prospective high school candidates.

Whenever I scheduled a school visit, I arranged a time through the counselor to meet interested students during the school day. I always asked the counselor to invite top juniors and seniors because I felt it could be helpful for the juniors to hear about highly selective colleges before senior year. The most progressive counselors would also invite top sophomores in the hopes that my presentation would encourage students to work hard and develop their talents. To have a group of 10 to 15 juniors and seniors in a small discussion session is both useful and educational. Smaller sessions with 2 to 4 seniors can be exceptionally valuable since the admissions representative can engage in a more personal conversation with the students.

I always took note of applicants who made positive or negative impressions during my visit, and I would review any notes on that candidate when I reviewed the applications from a given school. For example, one student from a public high school in Fort Worth, Texas, was particularly engaging during my school visit, asking poignant questions that were important to her as she considered the merits of leaving Texas for a college education. Her questions about life away from home, religious life on campus, and the premedical program at Harvard were thoughtful and relevant to her needs. There was little surprise when her application proved to be very strong and was accompanied by an incredible interview. At the other end of the spectrum, meeting students at a school can lead an admissions officer to identify students with marginal intrapersonal skills or students who may be less appealing from a personal perspective. I met one applicant at his high school in the northwest suburbs of Chicago the spring of his junior year, and though I was impressed with his level of interest in Harvard, I felt that he was pushy and hard-charging during my visit. While this would not be the ultimate strike against him, it confirmed the initial suspicions I had after reviewing his application. During his senior year, this candidate attended multiple recruiting events in the Chicago area and sent several follow-up letters repeating his interest in Harvard while complimenting staff members on their presentations. Although his case was strong by the numbers and by his activities, his interactions and communications with staff members left something to be desired. Ultimately he was not offered admission.

While high school visits provide the best opportunity for personal interaction, they are not always a success. Schedule conflicts, exams, and absences might keep some students from attending a visit, and the arrangements of the visit can create less than optimal conditions for interaction.

Most schools conduct College Fairs several times a year. Admissions liaisons are invited to tend a booth and speak with students who visit during the open period. College Fairs are reasonable venues for a visit so long as there is space for prospective candidates to sit down and converse with an admissions representative, but they also can be free-for-alls where less qualified and disinterested candidates monopolize admissions officers' time and deplete the supply of marketing literature as they reach for everything in sight. Pooling of resources can be a benefit to schools, students, and parents by bringing several high schools together for a program. It is cost effective for schools, and helps families share in the college search process together by exposing potential applicants to a variety of colleges.

Finally, some schools will only offer admissions officers a table inside or just outside the lunchroom due to school policies. This format was always my least favorite because students are in a hurry to eat lunch during their shortened free period, it's loud, and in some cases students may not even know that the representative is on campus. In order to visit many different schools over a period of years, however, I was always willing to try anything once. But I found it difficult to return to these types of settings when other schools were willing to provide more accommodating arrangements.

Over the course of a six-week fall recruiting schedule, I would split my travel time in a particular region according to the numbers of applications that had been received the previous year and past visits that had been made to the area. I've been responsible for the Fort Worth and Austin areas in Texas, the city of Chicago and its northern and western suburbs, select schools in the Boston area, and the states of Utah and Nevada. I would spend almost 50 percent of my travel time in areas that sent the largest number of applications—Chicago and Boston, for example. I typically recruited in Chicago for a week, and with Boston as my home base, I was fortunate to conduct two to three weeks' worth of school visits. Based on these travel commitments, I would spend two to three days in Utah, two days recruiting in the Austin and Fort Worth areas, and two days recruiting in Nevada.

Except for a few western states, most admissions recruiting is squeezed into a short window of seven to eight weeks between Labor Day and the first week in November. An admissions officer typically visits four to five high schools per day while on the road. Even if I'd been able to conduct visits for six full weeks, for instance, I could only have visited 125 schools out of the thousands that comprised my areas of responsibility. To augment school visits and help reach larger groups of students in a community, a variety of evening programs can be arranged, with hundreds or thousands of invitations sent throughout a region.

The Reading Process: Early Admission Whirlwind

The reading process at highly selective schools begins in earnest around the first of November, and it could not come at a better time. By the end of October admissions officers are worn thin by the intense travel schedules and are ready to begin reading about the candidates whom they've been meeting along the way.

With early admissions programs, there's not much time for staff members to recuperate from a long fall of recruiting. The early admissions cycle is a short six-week period that culminates with decision letters being mailed around December 15. In the time prior to Thanksgiving, admissions officers need to read and evaluate completed applications and request any missing or additional information from the candidate or school. Over the past seven years, early applications have soared at highly selective institutions. Although the percentage increase has slowed today, admissions offices report record numbers of applications every year. With the high school population continuing to increase through 2008, this trend is likely to continue unless there's a dramatic shift in the way early programs are administered.

Some highly selective schools see as much as 20 to 30 percent of their total applications in the early admissions process, but have less than one-third of the time to read and evaluate applications as they do for the regular admissions cycle. For schools that receive this high percentage of total volume, admissions readers log long hours well into the evening and morning for several weeks. Once

applications are read by the requisite number of admissions officers, the ratings are entered into a database that produces a candidate profile. At this point the ratings become as important as
documents in the application itself. Even as late information flows
in, admissions officers begin meeting in small committees to discuss the standout candidates in the pool. In committee, applications
are presented in the context of their schools, regions, and even areas
of the country or world.

Early admissions has such a short life cycle that committee
meetings have to be completed within a tight timeline. Along the
way, readers and committees try to assess one very important question in regard to any candidate who might be admitted early: Is this
person someone we *know* we would want to have in our class over
other strong choices who will be discussed in March? If the committee can't say yes without hesitation, the candidate will almost
certainly be deferred and placed in the regular application pool for
later comparison. Most applicants who apply to a highly selective
school will be deferred for review in the spring, but some applications will be denied admission early and hence cannot be considered in the spring admissions process.

The week following the early admissions mailing in December is
a busy one for the admissions staff, and probably the most intensive
and stressful period of the year. Many staff members speak over the
phone to parents and applicants who were deferred and are looking for ways to improve the application, and with deadlines lurking,
admissions officers need to pay particular attention to the details
without falling behind in the process. This is all the more critical
because the caliber of applicants in these early pools has shown an
incredible strength and depth in the past decade over those applying
through the regular admissions pool.

The Reading Process: April Admission and Rounding Out the Class

The January 1 admission deadline begins a much longer cycle that gives staffs the opportunity to delve more deeply into cases that may not have been quite as competitive in the "early" process.

January and February are used to retrieve mid-year grades and follow up on matters such as a student's RSI or Intel research paper, a candidate's sudden academic demise, or an individual's disciplinary record. It is much easier to contact counselors about a sudden drop in a student's grades or to discuss a slow start to another student's high school career when there are eight weeks of reading versus only three. Candidates' academic papers or research projects may be forwarded to faculty members for review. Applicants with supplementary materials such as a music tape are more likely to have these materials reviewed in the regular action time frame. Feedback and input from other sources allow admissions staffs to continue to make well-informed decisions for the remaining admissions slots.

This process also provides an opportunity for readers to review deferred early applications. Every year there are many applications that look stronger the second time around. For some, new information helps to elevate the strength of a case; for others, strengths stand out in comparison to the full applicant pool more than they did in the high-powered early group.

As an officer prepares to present cases, in both the early and the regular cycles, one has to think about the candidate individually, locally, and globally: How does he or she compare to current undergraduates? How does she compare with others from the same school and from previous admissions years with candidates from that school? How will he compare within the region, from coast to coast, and from around the globe?

Committee Meetings, Presenting Cases, Mailing Letters

Every school has its own way of presenting cases for admission. At some, the admissions officer makes recommendations and presentations to the dean, who is responsible for making the final decision. At other schools, decisions are made regionally by smaller teams, with senior staff members leading a committee process that results in initial admission recommendations for review by a larger body chaired by the dean of admissions and faculty members. In all of these cases, the primary admissions officer is required to determine the strongest candidates within schools and regions and be prepared to present and discuss his or her cases with the rest of the committee. The area admissions representative has the responsibility of knowing the quantitative and qualitative merits of the case, the strength of the curriculum and school system, the school application history, and other pertinent factors that could sway committee opinion.

Of course, many more cases will be discussed during this process than will actually be offered an admissions space. Presenting cases allows for competitive candidates to have their stories told and compared to other talented applicants. As more and more cases are presented, committee members can more accurately gauge where the "edge" of admission will be for a particular year. This "edge" is where the choices are made, and as cases are reviewed by committee members time and time again, leading candidates are identified.

Multiple reviews help build consensus during the process and narrow the field. By the time committee meetings reach March, many of the decisions have been made. However, there's still a great deal of fine-tuning that needs to occur late in the process. New information may elevate some cases and weaken others, thus repositioning the offers of admission. And the preliminary processes often approve more candidates for admission than the college can actually admit, sometimes by as many as several hundred students. In the last weeks of the process, these candidates are compared with the rest of the pool marked for admission. As the top candidates from Nepal are considered in the same context as a high-level "all-arounder" from Florida, a strong minority candidate from Harlem, or an outstanding musician from San Francisco, some of the cases most at the edge will be moved to the Waiting List or be denied admission entirely.

Making the final cuts is always the most difficult part of the process because 100 to 200 students who have made it "successfully" through the process will be cut from the admitted ranks on the last few days because there aren't enough spaces available in the class. For these students, the best hope for admission will be an offer from the Waiting List in May or June.

Once the letters are mailed to applicants during the first week of April, staff members turn their full attention to yield management and matriculation. Students have until May 1, the national signing date, to determine where they will attend college, and admissions offices utilize a number of recruiting tactics to draw students to their institution. Among them, they write personalized follow-up letters encouraging students to attend and offer visiting weekend programs in April, when admitted students can spend a weekend on campus meeting with students and faculty, visiting classes, and experiencing the social life of the campus. Admitted candidates may also receive calls from present students who offer to answer questions from a student perspective. Faculty members may contact truly outstanding prospects in their fields, and athletic coaches, music directors, or other mentors may choose to contact candidates with whom they've been communicating throughout the process.

At the end of the busy month of April, students have made their decisions. Now it's time to review candidates on the Waiting List, if necessary, and begin planning for the recruitment of the next wave of applications.

A Cruel Summer: Waiting on the Waiting List

With early admissions programs and other recruiting efforts, many highly selective institutions have become better equipped to manage the yield, or the percentage of admitted students, who will enroll after being offered admission. There are a finite number of dorm rooms and a predetermined class size, but the number of students who matriculate from year to year will still vary. Predicting the yield is, at best, a statistical art wherein the admissions committee is required to make a best estimate based upon the data available.

The Waiting List is primarily a tool for identifying students who would have been admitted had there been space available, but it is also used as way of acknowledging achievement of strong cases that might not be offered a space. There is a finite number of spaces, after all, and although those on the Waiting List were not accepted outright, highly selective universities would much rather admit students off this list to fill spaces when they become available than to put students in modular housing or pay for hotel rooms as dormitories in the case of overenrollment. Prior to Early Decision programs, even the most selective schools would admit upward of 200 applicants from the Waiting List. While a large number of candidates may still be admitted from the list, the number of spots offered has declined considerably in recent years.

Candidates placed on the Waiting List are usually informed of their status by the beginning of June, and admissions offices try to move quickly to admit the appropriate numbers of students based on available spaces. The remainder of the candidates will receive a letter informing them that they will not be offered a space in the class. The final group of students who remain on the Waiting List are those who are very interested in that particular college, and the admissions office would like to admit them if spaces become available later in the summer. These candidates should plan on attending another school in the fall with the hopes they'll receive a call by the end of June should a space become available.

The Waiting List is also an opportunity for admissions offices to test candidates' levels of interest in the university. Wait-listed students are asked to reply to the college and inform the admissions office if they would like to be considered for a space. Many students are excited about the prospects of attending a school that admitted them in April and will ask to be removed from the Waiting List. For those who wish to be considered, it helps the candidate to show a real interest in attending that school. I would suggest sending a personal e-mail or letter to the admissions representative for your region reiterating your desire to attend the school.

When it comes time to select students from the Waiting List, many admissions committees will be more likely to offer the space to a candidate who they know will attend than to someone who may not. While calling the school to ask if there's anything else you can do to enhance your case may seem like a reasonable direction, some schools discourage phone calls and prefer a sincere note showing interest in their university. Leave it to the admissions office to contact you by phone. If an admissions office wants to know more, you can be sure they'll be in touch.

APPLICATION PREPARATION: FROM MIDDLE SCHOOL TO COLLEGE

Early Awareness Makes a Difference

Some parents begin thinking about the prospect of college for their children at a young age. In fact, some candidates to highly selective schools begin preparing when they're 10 years old. It's important for parents to lay the foundations that will help cultivate and bring out the talents in their children. Students who receive significant resources and are exposed to a wide array of opportunities by involved parents have a good head start, but there is no specific preparation or planning that students and parents can do to guarantee admission to the school of their choice.

The extreme desire shown by some families to provide their children with outstanding educational resources in order to construct a "perfect" résumé for college is alarming and has engendered cynicism in many admissions offices. Intensive parental planning has become the norm rather than the exception for students. Parents are enrolling their children in test prep courses, and it's not unusual for parents to drive their kids to private counseling or participate in other activities designed exclusively to bolster their children's credentials in the eyes of an admissions officer. Most readers are aware of "packaged" applications, and they are off-putting to admissions professionals because the passions and quirks that make a candidate interesting get lost in the sterile packaging.

Still, it's undeniable that getting involved with a child's education early will have a positive impact on the college planning process. With solid study habits and sound direction, young students will be more self-directed and better prepared to make positive decisions that will have greater impact later in high school. There are a number of resources that can help students and parents start down the right path in preparing for college without having to invest a significant amount of money. Middle school is a good place for parents to instill good study habits and to start thinking about how choices made at this time might affect the development and growth of their children. I spent two years teaching math and science to seventh and eighth graders at a small Catholic school where too few parents paid close attention to the academic progress of their children. Middle school performance often has an impact on the course offerings that become available when these children enter high school.

Academic Planning: Grades 8 to 10

Placing the top students into the appropriate levels of rigor is never a problem for counselors and teachers, but it becomes more of a challenge for educators to find the right fit for late bloomers. This is where the involvement of parents can make the greatest impact. A key element in a child's future development, and one often overlooked by parents whose children are in eighth grade, is course selection. Speaking with teachers and counselors in middle school and requesting that your child be placed in a more rigorous program is not unreasonable. This opens communication between the school and the parents, which can only benefit the student in the long run, regardless of the academic path the student takes. In addition to the resources within the middle school, the Department of Education has developed resources and publications for middle school students and parents interested in learning more about college. You can visit their Web site (www.ed.gov) for more information or to request any of their publications.

Keep in mind that eighth grade is the transition from middle school to high school. As a parent, it is important to consider what comes next and make certain that your child is enrolled in an academic program that will adequately challenge him or her. The course selections parents and students make entering freshman year will not necessarily have a critical impact on final candidacy to college, but early choices can influence the level of rigor and the types of course offerings available to students later in high school.

Wherever possible, parents should seek to enroll their children in an appropriately rigorous freshman schedule. It's much easier to drop a level than to accelerate to more advanced classes in mid-year and play catch-up with the rest of the class. To be in a position to take AP classes as a junior or senior, it will be necessary to start on an appropriate track in ninth and tenth grades.

Guidance counselors work with teachers to plan students' academic schedules for the following year, and occasionally students are not placed into the appropriate courses or programs. While many private school systems have counseling offices that can accurately match students to their abilities, some public school counseling loads are enormous, making an individual assessment of a student's academic placement nearly impossible. In fact, the average counselor-to-student ratio nationwide is upward of 500 to 1. Ninth and tenth grade students get the least amount of college advising, since college advisers focus on juniors and seniors, and those counselors who are dedicated to ninth and tenth grade students often spend more time dealing with problems than anything else. Parents can better prepare their ninth and tenth grade children by attending parent-teacher meetings and encouraging counselors to register their children in more challenging academic programs. Some schools will conduct preparatory standardized testing for students at a younger age as well. Some gifted and talented programs even have middle school students sit for an early testing of the SAT I, but this isn't necessary.

If you're interested in getting familiar with the SAT I or ACT tests, I recommend considering the PSAT or the PLAN exams in tenth grade. These scores are not reported to college admissions offices, and the exams are structured in a manner similar to the SAT I and ACT, which are required for admission to college. Also, many highly selective colleges require three SAT II subject tests, which are subject specific and can be more challenging to the test taker; therefore, it's always best to take the exam upon completion of a class, while the content is fresh in the student's mind. If a student has taken the highest level of biology at the high school by the end of freshman year and is interested in studying the biological sciences in college, the SAT II in June of that year is the wisest choice. Since admissions offices consider the three best SAT II scores, there's no harm in taking SAT II tests as a freshman or sophomore.

Extracurricular Activities

Outside the classroom, there is a tremendous amount of opportunity for young high school students. Early involvement in extracurricular activities can build confidence, develop one's skills and talents, and provide opportunities for leadership. Sometimes the biggest challenge in becoming involved is the adjustment to high school and the variety of programs available to students in and out of the classroom. Ninth and tenth grade students are not necessarily expected to enter high school and instantaneously become the "Big Man on Campus," but finding a niche early in high school will better position them to turn that niche into a distinguishing trait and to evolve into a leader within that activity or organization.

It does not matter what you choose to do as long as you're involved and enjoy it. Nor does it make a difference whether the student chooses to participate in an organization at school or in the community. In either case, showing an early commitment gives students a better chance of finding an activity or a cause for which they are passionate. Extended commitment to and excitement about activities are worthy of note in the admissions process, and students who become engaged early stand a better chance of developing those passions into distinguishing features.

Participating in activities as a freshman and sophomore is also important because it shows that you did not decide to become involved once you realized in the spring of Grade 11 that you had very little extracurricular activities to discuss in your application. With so many different activities and programs sponsored by the school, admissions offices might wonder why a student would avoid getting involved. Extenuating circumstances or family commitments could certainly keep students from becoming significantly involved at school, but when those factors do not exist, questions will arise about how the candidate is going to contribute to campus life in college.

Junior Year: The Application Process

Ideally, by the junior year of high school the student will have thought about how to continue to develop his or her strengths, had some impact on their school or community, and will be considering college plans. Junior and senior years pass by quickly, and too often students do not actively begin to think about college until the summer preceding senior year. There are some important points that can keep you ahead of the process and potentially enhance your candidacy if you begin junior year:

> *Grades and course selection.* From an academic perspective, it's important that you are engaged in the most rigorous schedule possible. While grades matter throughout high school, the level of rigor and performance of your junior and first semester senior year are carefully examined. For students who have the opportunity, it's also a good time to enroll in at least one AP course. Students with AP courses on their transcripts and AP test results provide more substantive academic support in their college applications. Most schools today allow for juniors to take AP courses, so this is a less critical issue for many students than it once was.

> *SAT I and ACT.* Take the SAT I or the ACT in the winter or early spring of junior year, so you can make the appropriate

self-assessment of your performance. Most students take the exams in late spring of junior year, but that leaves far less time to put together a plan to help improve those scores. Tutoring or prep courses can be helpful, but don't invest your time or money until you know your baseline. Students are allowed to take the tests multiple times, and for the SAT I, admissions offices generally review only the best verbal and math scores. But I don't believe students should take either exam more than three times since very few students show significant improvement in their scores after three sittings, and certainly not a large enough improvement to impress an admissions committee. In fact, too many standardized tests could have a negative impact in the application process. Student applications with six or seven SAT I and ACT tests often suggest a level of intensity or perfectionism that may be considered extreme.

SAT II. By the time junior year ends, the student should complete a full repertoire of SAT II exams. Most of the highly selective schools require SAT II subject tests, often a mathematics exam and/or writing, and one advantage of taking three in the spring of junior year is that a full year's worth of subject matter is still fresh in the student's mind. In addition, the student can retake any SAT II exams in the fall of senior year if there's room for improvement.

Letters of Recommendation. There's a very good chance that your junior year teachers will know you as well as or better than your senior year teachers. Ask the teachers who you believe know you the best to write your letters at the end of junior year. With more time to reflect, your teachers will be better able to write personalized and more in-depth letters on your behalf.

In terms of extracurricular and personal development, there are far fewer general tactics to employ in preparation for applying to college. However, junior year is a big year for many students, since it's the first opportunity a student has as an upperclassman to assert leadership within the school. Do you hold or have you held any significant leadership positions, or have you won any recognition for your talents? Do others perceive you as someone who has made a positive impact on the school or your community? Awards and leadership are distinguishing signals for admissions officers, but time and commitment are just as valuable. The quality of the activities you've engaged in can be more important in the process than recognition.

While there are no absolutes in terms of the number of activities or the minimum time requirements, I would suggest that juniors engage in a minimum of 10 or more hours of involvement per week in order to build an extracurricular portfolio that will carry measurable weight in the admissions process.

Where Should I Apply?

By the spring semester of your junior year you will no doubt have developed your likes, dislikes, strengths, and weaknesses to a point where you can begin to match these interests and talents to colleges that might be a good fit for you. Use this as your first screening tool for finding the schools that are right for you. Remember that there are always multiple good matches, but the challenge is to find a place where you'll enjoy yourself and where you'll learn and grow during your four years.

Too often students choose to apply to colleges because they're brainwashed into believing they must apply to the most competitive and the most prestigious schools based on reputation rather than fit. Having a degree from a selective university may help open doors as you move forward in your career, but in the end the value of that degree can only be measured by how it is utilized during college and after graduation. Other candidates measure their college search by applying to schools where they believe they have the best chance of admission based upon their grades. While it's important to understand the admissions requirements for highly selective institutions, applicants should take these factors into account only after an initial wave of research.

When you start thinking about college and your expectations, you should focus on what you want most out of your education. Before you start addressing specific questions that you have about a particular college, ask yourself some basic but essential questions to give yourself an inventory of your interests. These should be the "big picture" questions regarding where you want to spend the next four years geographically, socially, culturally, and academically. Create a decision-making matrix (see Table 6-1) to help you prioritize the questions that are the most meaningful to you. If you can come up with 10 to 12 questions that are important to you and then answer them honestly, you'll be able to determine the schools where you'll most likely thrive.

After answering these questions you can start researching the schools that meet your criteria and narrow the list to a more targeted group of selective schools. High school college career centers, college Web sites, and college guidebooks can give you the building blocks for finding an initial list of schools. Web sites, such as The Princeton Review (www.review.com) and Peterson's (www.petersons.com) are also great all-in-one resources for parents and students to research schools in preparation for applying to colleges.

Table 6-1 *The Decision-Making Matrix*

Question	Answer	Importance 1. Extremely 2. Somewhat 3. Not Important	School(s) That Meet These Criteria	Notes
School Location/Setting				
Where is my ideal school located? In a large urban center (more than 250,000 people within the region)? In a small urban setting (population range 100,000 to 250,000)? In a suburban setting? In a rural or college town setting?				
What size undergraduate population interests you? (>10,000, 5000 to 10,000, 2000 to 5000, <2000)				
How far away from home are you interested in being (within a short drive, within a couple hundred miles, keep me on the same coast/time zone/get me as far away from home as possible)?				
School Features (Academic)				
What type of educational degrees/programs do I want the school to provide (Liberal Arts, Technical, Preprofessional, Co-op)?				
Can I receive a degree in my field(s) of interest? (List areas of study)				
What types of research opportunities are there for me?				

School Features (Nonacademic)				
What are the two most important activities I would like to continue in college?				
Define the campus culture or environment that appeals most to me.				
When I attend college, I want . . . to live on campus all four years, live off campus at some point, live in a fraternity or sorority or other?				
Am I interested in attending a school that has a diverse student body?				
Do I want to attend a school with a religious affiliation?				
Are there other cultural components that are important (military schools/academies, historically black colleges, etc.)?				
Personal Factors (Add only those questions that are truly important)				
	List schools that appear most frequently for "Extremely Important" questions			
	List schools that appear most frequently for "Extremely and Somewhat Important" questions			

Once you have this list, you need to start validating your choices by getting a feel for where you might stand in terms of the admissions process. This is where your analysis of admissions data, feedback from college counselors, and insights from college admissions representatives can help you devise a strategy. With a good self-assessment of your strengths and achievements, you should be able to develop a list of schools you will be glad to attend should you gain admission.

If finances do not prohibit your ability to travel, the spring of your junior year and the summer prior to senior year are the most opportune times for prospective candidates to experience college life firsthand. Visiting the campus can give students a feel for the energy and level of activity on campus. Summer college tours with your family or with touring groups are a great idea if you have the time, but you'll get more from the experience when classes are actually in session with full-time undergraduates. Though it may be difficult to schedule a fall trip in your senior year, when the college semester is under way, that would be the best time to get a feel for the campus.

If you have friends who attend certain colleges, you may want to schedule trips to visit them, sit in classes, or schedule an on-campus interview in the admissions office. You'll get to see the academic resources, residential life, and student offerings at the school, and you'll have a chance to interact with staff members who may eventually advocate on your behalf. But for those who can't afford to trek to the school and do not have friends who attend a school in which you have an interest, it should be noted that it is not essential to visit the campus. Often, admissions offices have programs where prospective candidates can talk or e-mail current students to hear more about attending the institution from a student's perspective.

Senior Year: Fine-Tuning Your Application

Senior year in high school is more about fine-tuning your application than about affecting change. With three full years on the transcript and a litany of activities under your belt, your last year becomes a balancing act between maintaining a high level of achievement and making the final decisions about college. Remember: First semester grades in your senior year matter. If your application teeters on the edge, admissions offices will call your counselor for the most recent senior grades. From an extracurricular perspective, you might want to consider focusing on the activities that are the most meaningful to you. By now you'll know what you most enjoy and which commitments have the most significance in your life, so there's no need to add a laundry list of activities during a busy senior fall.

The most important decisions and actions that occur senior year revolve around deciding where you'll ultimately apply to college. With thoughtful research and good advice from counselors and family members, you should be able to create a list of schools you would enjoy attending. Your chances for admission at some schools will be lower than at others, but you should still apply to a few "reach" schools. You can't be admitted if you choose not to apply, and it's all right to take the risk of being rejected as long as you have a solid range of schools on your application list. Although students tend to procrastinate and complete applications under the duress of deadlines, you can manage the process rather than have it manage you by staying organized.

- If you haven't asked teachers to write your Letters of Recommendation by the end of junior year, find willing teachers as early as possible senior year.

- Make sure you've completed at least one round of the standardized test requirements by November to leave flexibility should more tests be required.

- Use online applications or those that can be downloaded. Universities welcome them equally with the printed versions they mail. While applications need not be typed, handwritten applications should be written neatly with good penmanship.

- Always list your extracurricular activities in order of significance. If you choose to attach an extracurricular résumé, keep its length to one page for maximum effect.

- Be judicious with supplementary Letters of Recommendation or other supplementary materials. You do not want the most pertinent information in the application buried among superfluous "extras." Consult your counselor, teacher, or mentor before submitting additional materials.

- Write your short answers and essays in advance. Ask others to proofread them, but realize the limited role essays ordinarily play in highly selective admissions.

- Write to the schools you're most interested in attending, especially if you can't visit them in person. Some schools track interest levels closely, so it may help to send an interest letter as a follow-up to your application.

The Value of College Counseling

There are many more tips and personal details that will help you decide where to apply, but one of your best resources is your high school college counselor. The primary role of counseling offices is to handle the school's administrative side of the application process: to ensure that students take the appropriate standardized test scores for the varying admissions requirements at different colleges, and to produce an official academic record, signed and sealed for admissions offices. For many of the highly competitive colleges, counselors are also asked to write letters on behalf of the candidate and report on any serious disciplinary actions that may have been taken against a student.

Strong counseling offices also offer the student a valued and honest insight into the application process. They understand the requirements of selective colleges and have years of experience with students from their high school who have applied to these same universities in the past. Over time, based on their past students' experiences, counselors grasp the nuances in how different college admissions offices operate, and as a result, they can give solid advice to seniors.

In my years in admissions, counselors would also try to help students pull together an application strategy based upon a student's interests. The strategy balances the student's decision-making matrix for schools he or she is interested in attending against a rough estimate of the applicant's chances for admission at each school. A commonly used application strategy is to apply to two or three highly selective schools where the candidate might consider his chance for admission to be about 25 percent, two or three schools where the chances for admission are about 50 percent, and two schools where the chances for admission are 75 percent or higher. With this approach, applicants can play with the number of schools they apply to based upon the application fees they can afford, which can range from $35 to $65 per application, and the additional expense of standardized testing and campus visits. For example, there is an added expense to send

SAT I or SAT II score reports to more than the four colleges chosen during test registration. In all, applying to seven selective colleges costs about $500, excluding the costs of visiting campuses.

Outstanding counselors can take their expertise and professionalism to the next level through relationship building with admissions offices. As counselors establish themselves as credible and forthcoming representatives of the high school, admissions officers will turn to them for their professional and personal recommendation on the candidate. Even within poorly funded school systems there are caring and knowledgeable college advisers who understand the networking aspect of college admissions and work hard at advocating on behalf of their students. I always appreciated the efforts of the counselors at schools like Garfield High School in East Los Angeles, Lincoln Park High School in Chicago, and Paschal High School in Fort Worth, schools with limited staffing resources but that did a phenomenal job of advising and advocating on behalf of their students.

Relationship building, however, is a double-edged sword for high school counselors. While the first priority is to assist their students in gaining admission to college, counselors need the respect of admissions officers in order to advocate for future applicants. This means that counselors have to be able to differentiate between candidates within a group of students applying to the same university, and it's essential that they be truthful about issues that might influence an admissions committee's decision. A counselor's reputation is on the line when information is knowingly withheld, and counselors who are unable to keep an open line of communication with an admissions office will find fewer students gaining entry to those institutions in future years.

While a counselor's ability to bring helpful expertise to competitive admissions will vary from school to school, she is the only representative who builds relationships with admissions offices. There are many independent counselors for hire, who may claim to have close relationships with highly selective admissions offices, but these counselors are not well-received, so be cautious when considering hiring a private counselor. There may be other reasons to work with an independent counselor—such as test preparation, personal coaching, or more personalized school research—but private counselors can provide no guarantees for admission to highly selective schools based on their relationships with colleges.

Applying to College Early

Applying to highly selective colleges through an Early Action or Early Decision program has become commonplace in public high schools across the country, and in recent years it's been the standard for private secondary schools. Early programs were created originally to allow students to apply to a college by a November 1 deadline and receive an "early" notice about their admissions status around December 15. Early programs were marketed to give students the opportunity to apply to their first choice college early and get an indication of their admissions status in time to determine whether they should apply to other colleges for January deadlines. Over the last five years the sophistication and gamesmanship surrounding the early application process has generated a tremendous amount of attention from the media, parents, college counselors, and, most recently, university administrations.

Yale president Richard Levin has publicly questioned the value of Early Decision admissions programs, suggesting that it would be a "good thing" if all selective schools were to abandon such programs.[1] President Levin's commitment to change led to the announcement in November 2002 that Yale would return to offering an Early Action program, beginning with the 2003–2004 admissions year. Likewise, Stanford University is planning to switch from Early Decision to Early Action beginning with the class of 2008. Yale's decision and President Levin's focus on this issue may also encourage other universities to revisit their Early Admissions programs in order to bring about more stability, remove some of the confusion, and decrease the pressure and anxiety created during the early application process.

Where Early Decision requires a student to attend the institution, should the applicant gain admittance in December, Early Action is non-binding and allows students to apply to other schools for the regular January 1 deadline should they be admitted in December. This reduces the stress placed upon those who are admitted early. While there are still fewer selective schools that offer Early Action, Cal Tech, MIT, Georgetown, the University of Chicago, UNC-Chapel Hill, Boston College, Harvard, Stanford, and Yale provide prospective students the ability to apply to other schools in January even if the candidate is offered early admission.

Today, more highly selective schools implement Early Decision admissions over Early Action since these colleges are looking for students who (a) truly want to be on their campus, and (b) can help boost their yield statistics at the end of the admissions cycle. All of the other Ivy League schools—Duke, Northwestern, and Rice—and most of the "Small Ivy" schools, such as Amherst and Williams College, offer Early Decision programs.

Regardless of how colleges and universities present the merits of either program to prospective applicants, the early application process has an inherent conflict between serving the needs of the students and serving the needs of the institution. Colleges publicly spin the early admission program benefits as a way to provide students with flexibility and options, but early programs also create a competitive advantage for selective universities, particularly those schools that offer binding Early Decision. Offering choices to students was always a secondary goal of admissions offices, to admit top candidates early and increase the overall admitted student yield. Indeed, with early applicants tagging the selective schools as a first choice, in the case of Early Decision, or as a top choice, in the case of Early Action, these programs have evolved into a method of managing student matriculation rates. And because students who are admitted through early programs are more likely to attend that institution, the admit rates at those universities will drop.

In addition, this increased yield raises the "selectivity" of the institution, which is a highly valued and marketable statistic. Schools have effectively marketed low admissions rates to parents and students as a barometer of the standards of an institution. This recruiting ploy existed even before national college rankings began to exert an influence in the marketing wars, but the media frenzy has only exacerbated the desire of some selective schools to implement early decision to boost their "national" ranking. Most national guides and publications use selectivity as a significant measure for assessing the demand and value of schools for consumers, and savvy admissions administrators have used this measurement to their advantage.

Early Decision Considerations
for Schools

With the growth in popularity of Early Decision programs, there has been an increase in other challenging problems from the perspective of both the high school and the admissions offices. Many students now strategize about the early process in terms as a possible means of gaining acceptance early, versus choosing to apply to a college based upon the overall best match. Upward of 60 to 70 percent of the students who attend some private schools choose to apply to college through an early program, and at some schools the number can top 80 percent of the senior class. Many of these candidates are advised or decide that their best chances for admission are by declaring that a school is their first choice by applying Early Decision.

At several Ivy League and other Early Decision schools this assessment is in fact true. These colleges will admit "standard strong" students during the Early Decision process who well might not be admitted during the regular action period, because the candidate is committing to their school. Schools utilizing this admissions tactic run the risk of turning away stronger students in regular action because the number of spaces that can be offered is thereby reduced, which can affect admission of the best candidates. Students who receive less sophisticated advising, and students who are less influenced by the pressures and hysteria of applying early, may be put at a disadvantage at these schools.

What's more, those students who are concerned about financial aid—despite the fact that nearly all of these schools provide 100 percent need-based financial aid—may be less apt to apply for Early Decision for financial reasons. In the end, both the student and university are impacted by the tactic of pumping up the yield on admitted candidates by offering more admissions to early applicants. Great candidates who choose to wait until January may run the risk of being squeezed at an Early Decision university, and the universities may be sacrificing some quality in their student body for an increased commitment and yield from their students gained through a binding early program.

High school counselors in schools that have seen students admitted to college through early admissions programs have noticed an increase in the number of students whose academic performance wanes significantly once they've been admitted early. Very few admissions offices will pay attention to first semester grades after December 15, let alone third term senior grades, and some students are taking advantage of this and coasting through the remainder of the academic year. To go from a straight A record to a mixed bag that includes C grades should warrant a letter from the college asking for a letter of explanation. I am not advocating that hundreds of offers be rescinded, but I think it's crucial for colleges to inform students that they are accountable for their actions and could lose a place in the class for serious indifference to their academic responsibilities. Senior high school teachers and counselors want senior year to matter, and admissions offices must support them by watching senior year grades more carefully. Having taught in a high school for two years, I understand just how difficult it can be to teach once "senior slide" sets in. With early admissions, unfortunately, the slide can hit as early as December.

Given the rapid shift toward early programs, admissions offices face demographic challenges. Historically, the demographic of early programs tended to be largely comprised of upper-middle-class white and Asian applicants from affluent suburban public and private schools. It is hard to build a particularly diverse class when so many of the candidates share similar backgrounds and experiences. A second and more practical problem that has risen is the sheer number of applications that need to be reviewed in a six-week period. Early Action schools are hit particularly hard with more students per school applying to Early Action programs than Early Decision schools because they do not need to commit to attending that institution. With so many students from a similar demographic choosing to apply early, some admissions offices are starting to question the role of early programs in admission altogether. The intensity and gamesmanship that students, parents, and schools have implemented in the process has taken away from the original advantages of these programs.

From a recruiting and marketing perspective, some selective admissions offices will not be interested in dropping an Early Decision program. Increased selectivity has raised their yield and lifted their national rankings, and in fact, several schools believe that Early Decision has helped improve the quality of the student body. What incentive is there for UPenn, Duke, or Dartmouth to move away from Early Decision when there are strategic benefits for continuing to offer candidates such a program? Universities with low admissions rates and high yields, such as Harvard, Princeton, Stanford, and Yale, could afford to end their early programs to bring some order back to the process and hold students academically responsible for the majority of senior year. For other top schools, however, the competitive marketing advantage Early Decision offers would be eliminated, forcing these admissions offices to walk away from programs that improve their recruiting efforts! Without Early Decision, some schools would have a more difficult time predicting how many students would decide to attend their university, and admissions rates would increase without any benefit for the admissions office other than a more complete academic transcript.

It will be interesting to see how the Early Decision landscape will change over the next few years. I suspect it will be difficult for a large number of selective schools to agree on a policy that works reasonably well for everyone. Until change is brought about, candidates who find a school they like should strongly consider applying early, especially if their credentials are in the "standard strong" range according to admissions standards. Although applying to an Early Decision school reduces an applicant's college options in senior year, the application may get the tip that it needs at some schools to ensure admission.

A Note on Financial Aid

While this book is not designed to specifically discuss financial aid, it's difficult to talk about admissions without considering the financial ramifications of applying to a highly selective institution. Students and their families should be concerned about the escalating costs of an undergraduate education, where the cost of attending most of the highly selective institutions has exceeded $30,000 per year. However, there are several reasons why the cost of an institution should not prohibit anyone from applying to a highly selective school.

First, almost all highly selective schools have continued to support 100 percent need-based financial aid for students and families. This means that the institutions will assist students in funding a college education with scholarships or grant money as well as low-interest student loans. In looking at the numbers, 40 to 70 percent of the students at highly selective institutions have financial aid of some sort.

Second, competition between the top universities has fueled a buyer's market for students. State university systems have developed appealing merit awards to keep top in-state talents at the leading public research institutions. The University of Virginia and UNC-Chapel Hill have been offering outstanding merit programs for years. In addition, private colleges such as Rice, Emory, Duke, and Northwestern have a small number of enticing full merit programs to attract a handful of elite applicants each year. Ivy League schools, all which offer to meet 100 percent financial need, provide no merit awards, but compete for top talent by focusing on the indebtedness of their students upon graduation. Princeton recently decided that no undergraduate would be required to take out a student loan to attend Princeton, and other Ivy schools have responded by reducing the annual expected level of loans students are required to take. With this type of competitive marketplace, students will be able to more easily afford the nation's top colleges. All of these changes will benefit the consumer, and you can always choose to attend another, more generous institution if a college cannot meet what you or your family can afford to pay.

Students and parents interested in learning more about financial aid and scholarship opportunities independent of university financial aid programs should start by scouring the resources available in college counseling offices and on the Internet. The Department of Education (www.ed.gov) is a comprehensive resource on financing a college education. Finaid (www.finaid.com) is another resource that can help educate students and parents about paying for a college education, and Fastweb.com (www.fastweb.com) is a resource designed to help students search for appropriate scholarship opportunities. Given the current direction of university financial programs and the possibilities for students to receive scholarships and low-interest loans, the prospects for students to afford highly selective educations look bright.

Endnotes

1. Karen W. Arneson, "Yale Proposes That Elite Colleges Abandon Early Decision Admissions," *New York Times*, Education section, December 13, 2001.

PART III

HARVARD
CASE STUDIES

AN EXAMINATION OF ADMISSIONS APPLICATIONS

Case study reviews, long a valuable tool for learning about the decision-making process in business, is also one of the best ways for understanding the choices admissions offices make. Examining, from an admissions offices' perspective, the applications of a sample of students admitted to some of the most selective schools, will reveal the challenges of evaluating the individual merits of candidates within the framework of an institution's needs.

An array of factors shape the decision-making process, and the five cases presented here have been chosen to offer insight into the dynamics involved. For these five applicants admitted to Harvard between 1996 and 1998, the original applications, as best recalled by the students, include accurate school, demographic, and background information. All were solid, admissible "choices," but none were Clear Admits. None of them had standardized SAT test scores in the top 25 percent of the Harvard admitted class, which generally begins at 1560 to 1570 or higher, depending on the year. In several cases it took extensive committee discussion prior to making the ultimate decision to offer admission.

I'll present the data components of their applications and a list-ing of their achievements, backgrounds, and high school experi-ences. You'll see the positive factors that influenced the admissions discussion—the elements that helped tip the scales in each of these applicants' favor. Other valuable information, such as essays, teacher letters, interview reports, and transcripts were unavailable for these case studies, but the data provided here is a solid basis for understanding how admissions officers consider a candidate.

In addition to examining the applications and factors that pre-pared the way for their admission, the five cases look at the accom-plishments of these students during and after college. This analysis adds an unusual perspective to the concept of the "futures test" and how the admissions committee looks beyond the college years to the candidates' contributions to society as alumni.

Read the cases as if you were part of an admissions committee, and ask yourself probing questions about the candidate based on what you see in the application. What are the candidate's strengths? How might the candidate make an impact on the campus? What parts of the application make the case compelling or vulnerable in the admissions process? In addition to looking at the individual merits of the case, evaluate the candidates collectively. If you were part of a decision-making committee at a highly selective university, would you select any of these candidates? How would you vote, if there were only two admissions spaces for the five applicants? While admissions offices rarely, if ever, have to choose among such a small pool of candidates, consider how difficult it is to select the final 50 or so candidates out of the last several hundred strong cases identified by the committee to be compared and chosen.

Case Study 1: Kelly

Regular Action Applicant

School:
Dedham High School

Description: Public, suburban high school with a comprehensive curriculum. Nine AP courses offered; 68% of graduates attend four-year colleges, 17% attend two-year colleges, and 15% pursue employment, military or other.

Mother: Bank Teller

College: none

Father: Police officer, Town of Dedham

College: none

Siblings: sister, 23; sister 17

First Language, if not English:

Ethnicity: White

Tentative Field of Study:
Biology

Commitment: 2 (1–5 scale; 1 = absolutely certain, 5 = undecided)

Intended occupation: Medicine

Commitment: 1 (1–5 scale; 1 = absolutely certain, 5 = undecided)

College activities: journalism and field hockey

Commitment: 1 (1–5 scale; 1 = absolutely certain, 5 = undecided)

Class Rank: 2/160

SAT I: V-750, M-710

SAT II: Writing, 730; Math IC, 680; Chemistry, 670

List cities and countries where you have lived, with years of residence in each:

Dedham, MA, 17 years

Advance Placement/IB results and courses to be taken:

Twelfth grade, to be taken: Biology, English Comp/Lit, Calculus AB

Activities/Honors

Extracurricular Activities	Years/Grades of Participation	Office/Position(s) Held and Year
HS Newspaper	10, 11, 12	Editor in chief (12)
Student Government	10, 11, 12	Student rep
Senior Class Play, actress		
Athletics		
Varsity Field Hockey	10, 11, 12	
Varsity Track and Field	10, 11, 12	
Academic/Other Honors		
Wellesley College Book Award	11	
Dedham HS Distinguished Graduate of the Year	12	
National Honor Society	11, 12	
Employment		
Snack bar attendant	Summer 1996	
Day care provider	Summer 1994	

Summary of the Case

- Local applicant with strong grades and test scores.
- Can probably do well in the biology/medicine area.
- Noncollege/blue-collar background (NC/BC) is appealing.

- Police officer father adds a plus to background tip.

- Attends a decent school not known for regularly producing these types of test scores.

- Accomplished in ECA and athletics and is a "best of" all-around candidate from the school and area.

Pause Factor(s)

- Though a strong school presence, does not have a nationally distinguishing excellence in comparison to others in the pool.

- Interest in medicine is genuine but not unusual in the applicant pool.

- School support and interview will have to elevate this case to solidify a spot.

Ratings Profile

> *Academic:* Edge of Level 2 (possible Magna/Honors).

> *Extracurricular:* Strong Level 2 (regional/school leader).

> *Personal and school support:* Level 2: both areas were rated very strong. Kelly was praised for her warmth, positive energy, and commitment to the school and the town.

Final Review. All of the tip factors, including background, proximity to Harvard, and a compelling interview helped push this all-around candidate through regular action as a **Regular Action Admit**.

College and Beyond

Academics. Kelly graduated from Harvard in 2001 with a degree in History of Science—Magna cum Laude honors. Her senior thesis received a "Magna plus" rating by the faculty with a thesis titled,

"George Montandon and French Racialism: Theory and Practice, 1935–1944." She completed all of the prerequisite courses and examinations for medical school and is planning on applying after a year of full-time work.

Extracurricular

Housing and Neighborhood Development program (HAND) volunteer, dedicated to the community service programs in Cambridge and Greater Boston.

Kuumba Singers member. The Kuumba Singers celebrates the genius of black music through various forms of music, including spirituals, gospel, African folk, and other forms of artistic expression.

Employment/Future Plans/Comments. Kelly recently worked for a small company that manages seven nonprofit associations for financial service professionals and estate planners while she prepared to apply to medical school. She has the caring and warmth of personality that will make her a phenomenal doctor committed to serving those in working-class communities.

Case Study 2: Alex

Regular Action Applicant

School:
The Webb School of California

Description: Private boarding and day school with a comprehensive curriculum boys' education with coeducational opportunities. More than 15 AP courses offered; 100% of graduates attend four-year colleges.

Mother: Homemaker

College: none

Father: Teacher

College: LSU, bachelor's; Cal State LA, teaching certificate

Siblings: brother, 23; brother 9

First Language, if not English:
Spanish

Ethnicity: Mexican American

Citizenship: Dual citizen with Mexico

Tentative field of study:
Social Studies

Commitment: 2 (1–5 scale;
1 = absolutely certain,
5 = undecided)

Intended occupation:
Government/Politics

Commitment: 2 (1–5 scale;
1 = absolutely certain,
5 = undecided)

College activities: water polo, student government, ethnic and multicultural groups

Commitment: 3 (1–5 scale;
1= absolutely certain,
5 = undecided)

Class rank: 92%/37

SAT I: Verbal, 640; Math, 620

SAT II: Spanish, 800; U.S.History, 690; Writing, 680

List cities and countries where you have lived, with years of residence in each:

Mexico City, 12 years; Riverside, CA, 7 years (since 1991)

Advance Placement/IB results and courses to be taken:

English Comp/Lit 4, U.S. History 4; To be taken: French Literature, Physics B, European History

Activities/Honors

Extracurricular Activities	Years/Grades of Participation	Office/Position(s) Held and Year
Student Government	10, 11, 12	Class President (12) Class VP (10)
A Better Chance, Inc	10, 11, 12	Leadership Council
School Orchestra	10, 11, 12	Concertmaster
Latino Alliance	9, 10, 11, 12	President (10, 11, 12)
Model U.N.		
Athletics		
Varsity Water Polo	10, 11, 12	Captain (12)
Junior Varsity Soccer	10, 11	
Academic/Other Honors		
Claremont Rotary Club— "Americanism in Action" award	11	
Water Polo MVP	12	
Cum Laude Society		
Summer Programs		
Phillips Andover Academy summer session	Summer 1995	
LEAD— University of Arizona	Summer 1997	

Personal Essay (excerpt). Following are the opening and closing paragraphs of Alex's essay.

Although I lived in Mexico for the first 12 years of my life, nothing prepared me for the cultural shock I experienced this summer when I visited a maquilador plant in Nogales, Mexico. We toured the plant, which recycled old copy machine and printer cartridges. The plant operated as expected: some workers busily cleaned cartridges in the line, some filled these with new ink, and others packed them into marked cardboard boxes. The machines and the people worked busily just as in an American manufacturing plant. However, the atmosphere of this Mexican maquiladora plant was rich with tension; tension between the management and the workers. This conspicuous tension, evinced in the silence of the Mexican workers and the coldness of the American management, was due to the wage discrepancy between the former and the latter.

In my pursuit to comprehend the many factors—both in politics and economics—that contribute to the system of the maquiladoras, I became interested in international relations, particularly in those of the U.S. with Latin America. I lived in Mexico City for most of my life and I understand both the American and Mexican cultures, and their languages and traditions. Although I have also been interested in their politics and economies, it was not until this summer when I experienced the above that I decided to turn this interest to a life-long pursuit. I plan to study Economics at Harvard, and perhaps law afterwards, in order to begin accomplishing my goal and fulfilling my promise.

Summary of the Case

- Solid academic applicant from a good private school in Southern California. Few applications received from the Riverside area of greater L.A.

- Teaching family background a plus.

- Mexican American background from Southern CA with dual citizenship a plus.

- SAT II scores are better than SAT I scores and grades prove he can flourish at Harvard academically.

- Accomplished in ECA and athletics at small school.

- Essay is not without flaws but gives added depth to his background and interests. Essay also supports his academic and career goals well.

Pause Factor(s)

- Scores, aside from Spanish SAT II, are standard to modest for Harvard candidate.

- Big fish in a small pond. Will he make as much impact at Harvard as he has at Webb?

- Mr. Everything at this small school, but are his accomplishments less significant in comparison to others with similar leadership positions at large public schools?

Ratings Profile

> *Academic:* Level 3 (solid, possible Honors).
>
> *Extracurricular:* Strong Level 2 (regional/school leader).
>
> *Personal and school support:* Level 2: Support in application and interview were strong, and college counselor, respected

by the admissions committee, gave exceedingly strong support of Alex.

Final Review. As a school leader who was on scholarship at an affluent private school, his accomplishments impressed the committee. Family background and geographic tip were important factors, while school testimony told the committee that this was an engaging, highly motivated person who would add much to college life and follow through on his international politics and economics interest. **Regular Action Admit**.

College and Beyond

Academics. Concentrating in Economics with a certification in Latin American Studies, A.B. expected in January of 2003. Thesis Topic: Acquisition of Mexican banks by foreign financial institutions.

Studied abroad at Universidad de las Americas-Puebla, fall semester 2000.

Extracurricular

Varsity Water Polo, 1998, 1999, 2001.

Saturday Success Tutor. Volunteer tutor for Boston area middle school on Saturday mornings.

Hacia Democracy. Business director of student-led organization that promotes democracy and free markets in Latin America through an annual pan-American Model Organization of American States (OAS) for high school students, 2001–present.

Term-time work, 15 hours/week.

Employment/Summer Experience/Comments

Sloan School of Management, MIT. Research assistant, summer 2001–present.

U.S. House of Representatives. Legislative research assistant for Rep. Solomon Ortiz (TX-D) through Congressional Hispanic Caucus Institute, summer 1999.

Upon graduation, Alex plans to pursue a career in international business focusing on Central or South America and accepted a position with Lehman Brothers in January 2003.

Case Study 3: Jennifer
Early Action Applicant

School: Patrick Henry HS and Roanoke Valley Governor's School

Description: Public, small city school in rural region with a comprehensive program. Students may apply to attend Governor's School for Science and Technology in addition to main schooling; multiple AP courses offered. 65% of graduates attend two- or four-year colleges

Mother: Photographer

College: UT-El Paso, bachelor's; Hollins College, master's

Father: Lawyer

College: Harvard, bachelor's; Washington and Lee, J.D.

Siblings: brother, 16; brother, 13

First Language, if not English:

Ethnicity: White

Other Languages: Spanish

Tentative field of study: Humanities

Commitment: 2 (1–5 scale; 1 = absolutely certain, 5 = undecided)

Intended occupation: Arts

Commitment: 1 (1–5 scale; 1 = absolutely certain, 5 = undecided)

College activities: debate, drama, and the arts

Commitment: 3 (1–5 scale; 1 = absolutely certain, 5 = undecided)

Class rank: 1/325

SAT I: Verbal, 720; Math, 680

SAT II: Spanish, 780; Writing, 740; Math I, 700

List cities and countries where you have lived, with years of residence in each: Roanoke, VA:

1981–present (16 years); St. Croix, U.S. Virgin Islands: 1979–1981 (2 years)

Advance Placement/IB results and courses to be taken:

AP Spanish 5; To be taken: U.S. History

Activities/Honors

Extracurricular Activities	Years/Grades of Participation	Office/Position(s) Held and Year
Policy Debate	11, 12	
Spanish Tutor	11, 12	
Red Cross Volunteer	9, 10, 11	
Beta Club	11, 12	
Athletics		
Varsity Swimming	10, 11, 12	
Varsity Tennis	9, 10	
Academic/Other Honors		
Harvard Book Award	11	
Glenbrooks National Debate Tournament—Semifinalist	11	
Top Speaker, 1st place UVA National Debate Tournament	11	
Top Speaker and finalist, UGA National Debate Tournament	11	
Spanish National Honor Society	9, 10, 11, 12	President (12)
Summer Programs		
Stanford National Debate Institute	Summer 1996	
Governor's School for Humanities	Summer 1996	
Governor's Spanish Academy	Summer 1995	

Staff Interview. I was the area admissions officer for Jennifer when she applied to Harvard, and I had the opportunity to spend time getting to know the candidate during my fall recruiting visit to schools in the area. She was charismatic, full of energy, and had a talent and penchant for the visual arts and debate. Her academic and extracurricular plans for college were clear to her, and it was evident from my interview that Jennifer would pursue interesting areas of study in college and be a dynamic force on campus.

Summary of the Case

- Regional argument for case, since southwestern Virginia (west of Charlottesville) does not regularly send admits to Harvard.

- Wants to pursue Visual and Environmental Studies, a small concentration at Harvard worth supporting.

- Alumni tip is strong on this case, as her father had been a long-time interviewer for the admissions office.

- Strong SAT II scores and facility in Spanish (SAT II 780, AP 5) bolstered the academic case.

- Debating is a strong niche—she is accomplished at a national level.

Pause Factor(s)

- Probably won't debate in college, so some might wonder where she plugs in at Harvard aside from film interests.

- Lineage background adds to case but slightly weakens the regional or "area" argument for the case.

- She applied Early Action. Would she be assured a space in April?

Ratings Profile

Academic. Edge of Level 2 (possible Magna/Honors).

Extracurricular. Strong Level 2 (regional/school leader).

Personal and school support. Level 2: both areas were rated incredibly strong.

Final Review. Debate accomplishments, regional argument with strong lineage tip, valedictorian status, strong Spanish scores, and her interest in the entertainment industry helped to propel Jennifer into the class as a strong **Early Action Admit**.

College and Beyond

Academics. Graduated from Harvard in 2001 with a degree in Visual and Environmental Studies, Magna cum Laude honors. Senior film project focused on an adaptation of a Raymond Carver story.

Extracurricular

Harvard Entertainment Association. President and cofounder.

Harvard Advocate (literary magazine founded in 1866). Film Festival creative direction and developer, 1999 and 2000.

College Employment

Harvard Alumni Office. Business Schools Reunion Coordinator (term-time four years).

Disney Studios. Summer internship, 2000.

Employment/Future Plans/Comments. Jennifer was an incredibly active student in the film and media world at Harvard. Jennifer presently lives in Los Angeles and has worked at a production company as an assistant to a producer and presently works at New Line Cinemas.

Case Study 4: Justin

Regular Action Applicant

School: Westlake High School

Description: Public, large suburban school west of Austin, Texas. Upper-middle-class community with a comprehensive program. More than 13 AP courses offered; 83% of graduating seniors attend four-year schools, 11% attend two-year schools, and 6% pursue employment, military, or other.

Mother: Teacher

College: UT–Austin

Father: Business, Rancher

College: UT–Austin; St. Mary's University, JD

Siblings: brother, 25; sister, 17

First Language, if not English:

Ethnicity: White

Other Languages: Spanish

Tentative field of study: Humanities

Commitment: 1
(1–5 scale;
1 = absolutely certain;
5 = undecided)

Intended occupation: Business

Commitment: 3
(1–5 scale;
1 = absolutely certain,
5 = undecided)

College activities: football and baseball

Commitment: 1
(1–5 scale;
1 = absolutely certain.
5 = undecided)

Class rank: 22/475

SAT I: Verbal, 580; Math, 730

SAT II: Math IC, 650; Writing, 590; U.S. History, 570

List cities and countries where you have lived, with years of residence in each:

Austin, TX: 1994–present (4 years); Fort Worth, TX: 1980–1994 (14 years)

Advance Placement/IB results and courses to be taken:

Spanish 4, English Lang/Comp. 3; To be taken: Spanish Lit., U.S. History

Activities/Honors

Extracurricular Activities	Years/Grades of Participation	Office/Position(s) Held and Year
Piano	9, 10, 11, 12	
Fellowship Christian Athletes	11, 12	
Athletics		
Varsity Football	10, 11, 12	
Varsity Baseball	11, 12	
Academic/Other Honors		
National Honor Society	11, 12	
State Finalist—FCA Athlete of the Year	12	
Football—All State Honorable Mention, 1st team All-Central Texas	12	
Football—State Champions	11	
Baseball—1st team All Central Texas	11	
Summer Programs and Employment		
Spain summer school and travel	Summer 1996	
Restaurant waiter	Various	
Ranch work	Summer 1997	

Staff Interview. I was the area admissions officer for Justin when he applied to Harvard, and I had the opportunity to interview him on his football-recruiting trip to Cambridge. He was a genuinely nice person with a respectful "yes sir/no sir" Texas demeanor. He impressed me with his commitment to his piano and religious activities in addition to his rigorous athletic schedule.

Summary of the Case

- Top football recruit with admissible academic credentials.

- The ranching background adds appeal, though not considered a more rural ranching family.

- Piano skills impressed the committee by showing a different side to his personality.

- Top 5 percent in one of the better public high schools in Texas, and Spanish AP helps case.

- The interview helps Justin pass the "broken leg" test as a candidate who would be a good roommate and add to campus life, even if he did not participate in a varsity sport.

Pause Factor(s)

- Scores are inconsistent and writing scores are weak, near the edge of admission.

- Some concern with what he might add to the campus if he is unable to play football.

- School support lauded personal qualities but did not place him in the top tier academically.

Ratings Profile

   Academic. Level 4 (fair to marginal for Harvard).

Extracurricular. Level 1 (varsity football recruit).

Personal and school support. Level 2 and Level 3: high for personal qualities, average for academic potential, with strong admissions interview.

Final Review. Math scores, grades, and Spanish AP were solid enough, helping to overcome weaker verbal credentials as a national athletic recruit with outstanding personal qualities. Staff interview sealed the case, as the committee felt he had a breadth of talents to pass the "broken leg" test. **Regular Action Admit**.

College and Beyond

Academics. Justin graduated from Harvard with an AB in Psychology in June 2002.

Extracurricular

Harvard Varsity Football, free safety. Two-year letter winner and four-year team member. Undefeated Ivy League champions in 2001.

Employment/Future Plans/Comments. Even at Harvard, football was a 30- to 40-hour-per-week commitment in the fall semester and a 20-hour-per-week commitment in the spring. Spring semester senior year, Justin considered several business options upon graduation, including opportunities in South Texas and Mexico and his father's ranching business and angus beef operations.

Case Study 5: Nancy

Early Action Applicant

School: Boston Latin School	**Tentative field of study:** Social Studies
Description: Public; large urban, exam school. Highly diverse school with comprehensive academic program. 25 AP courses offered, but level of academic rigor varies in school.	**Commitment:** 4 (1–5 scale; 1 = absolutely certain, 5 = undecided)
	Intended occupation: Social service
Mother: Laundromat, part-time assistant	**Commitment:** 3 (1–5 scale; 1 = absolutely certain, 5 = undecided)
College: none	**College activities:** social service and journalism
Father: Sales representative	
College: none	**Commitment:** 1 (1–5 scale; 1 = absolutely certain, 5 = undecided)
Siblings: brother, 21; sister, 20	**Class rank:** 19/360
First Language, if not English: Chinese	**SAT I:** Verbal, 730; Math, 670
Ethnicity: Asian American	**SAT II:** Writing, 730; Biology, 650; Math IC, 640

List cities and countries where you have lived, with years of residence in each:

Boston (Allston-Brighton), MA: entire life. Family immigrated to the U.S. from Hong Kong two months before Nancy was born.

Advance Placement/IB results and courses to be taken:

English Lang/Comp 4, Latin (Virgil) 3; To be taken: Euro History, Statistics, Biology, English Literature, U.S. History, Latin Literature

Activities/Honors

Extracurricular Activities	Years/Grades of Participation	Office/Position(s) Held and Year
School Newspaper	9, 10, 11, 12	Editor in chief (12)
Student Magazine	9, 10, 11, 12	Associate editor (12)
Drama Club	9, 10, 11	Producer
Key Club	9, 10, 11, 12	
Asian-American Student Association	9, 10, 11, 12	
Band	9, 10, 11, 12	1st Clarinet All-State (11)
Academic/Other Honors		
Columbia University Book Award	11	
Massachusetts State Science Fair, 1st place	12	
NE Scholastic Press Association, Certificate of Excellence	12	
Summer Programs		
MA State Senate, Legislative Intern	Summer 1996	
Teaching Assistant, UMass Boston	Summer 1995	
Simmons College	Summer 1996	

Staff Interview. Nancy had several outstanding interviews. As a Boston public schools candidate, she was invited to interview in the admissions office with the area admissions officer. All indications from those who knew her suggested she had the drive, energy, and resilience to handle Harvard's demands with flying colors.

Summary of the Case

- Nancy was an extracurricular whirlwind and made an impact on the school.
- NC/BC background appeal even stronger with her first-generation upbringing as the daughter of an immigrant family.
- Solid verbal skills and not interested in studying in her areas of weakness (math/science).
- Incredible support from school.

Pause Factor(s)

- Weak math/science scores.
- Class rank of 19 at BLS is near the low edge for admitting a student to Harvard from this school.
- Would she be able to balance her academic schedule with her extracurricular plans?

Ratings Profile

  Academic. Level 3 (solid, possible Honors candidate).

  Extracurricular Level 2 (strong regional/school).

  Personal and school support. Level 1: Rare personal qualities. Headmaster of the school praised her, and staff interview cited special qualities as well.

Final Review. Attending Boston public schools a huge plus, as the university looks carefully at Cambridge and Boston residents. In her case, Nancy lived in Brighton, a part of Boston where some of Harvard's campus sits, making her case even more compelling. However, the academic match was enough of a question that Nancy was deferred in Early Action. Her first semester senior grades were excellent and moved her class rank to 13th. Combined with her accomplishments, family background, staff interview, and a rising transcript, Nancy was offered a space in the class of 2001 during the regular admissions process. Regular Action Admit.

College and Beyond

Academics. A.B. English Language and American Literature, 2001.

Extracurricular

Harvard Alumni Association David Alioan Prize. Given to two seniors who have made the most significant contributions to residential life.

Laura Houghteling Memorial Fellowship. Merit scholarship given to seniors for graduate study because of promise of future contributions to society.

Dunster House Committee, co-chair 2000–2001.

Harvard-Radcliffe varsity crew. Coxswain; national bronze medalist, NCAA Academic All-American, Academic All-Ivy.

Early College Awareness Programs. Undergraduate coordinator (junior, senior) to tutor, mentor middle school students in preparation for high school and college.

Community Service. Chinatown Committee volunteer, HARMONY music teacher.

Employment/Future Plans/Comments. Nancy is presently enrolled in a joint master's degree program through the Harvard Graduate School of Education and the Harvard Kennedy School of Government. She is studying education and public policy issues affecting underprivileged students and spent three weeks in the summer of 2002 studying in an international program in Hong Kong.

Nancy's energy in high school followed her to college, and she made a huge contribution to Harvard campus life and the Cambridge and Boston communities. Her accomplishments were recognized by the university, which awarded her a Harvard Pforzheimer Fellowship, a merit award to continue studying in any of the Harvard graduate schools.

APPENDIX

Table A-1 *Determining a Converted Rank Score (CRS) Using Formula*
(Calculate for Y when absolute class rank is given)

$$Y = \frac{(2 \times \text{Absolute Rank}) - 1}{2 \times \text{Class Size}}$$

Y	CRS	Y	CRS	Y	CRS
0.0017	80	0.1712	60	0.8531	40
0.0023	79	0.1978	59	0.8749	39
0.0031	78	0.2267	58	0.8944	38
0.0041	77	0.2579	57	0.9115	37
0.0055	76	0.2913	56	0.9265	36
0.0072	75	0.3265	55	0.9394	35
0.0095	74	0.3633	54	0.9505	34
0.0123	73	0.4014	53	0.9599	33
0.0159	72	0.4405	52	0.9678	32
0.0203	71	0.4802	51	0.9744	31
0.0257	70	0.5199	50	0.9798	30
0.0323	69	0.5596	49	0.9842	29
0.0402	68	0.5987	48	0.9878	28
0.0496	67	0.6368	47	0.9906	27
0.0607	66	0.6736	46	0.9929	26
0.0736	65	0.7088	45	0.9946	25
0.0886	64	0.7422	44	0.9960	24
0.1057	63	0.7734	43	0.9970	23
0.1252	62	0.8023	42	0.9978	22
0.1470	61	0.8289	41	0.9984	21
				1	20

Note: Round value of Y to next highest decimal found in the table to find CRS. Example: 0.0099 rounds up to 0.0123, thus giving a CRS of 73.

Example: Class rank is 17 out of class of 416.

$$Y = \frac{(2 \times 17) - 1}{2 \times 416} = \frac{33}{832} = 0.0397, \text{ which rounds up to } 0.0402 \text{ or a CRS of } 68$$

Table A-2: *General Conversion Table to Determine a CRS from GPA, Percentile, or Other Conventional Grading System*
(Use the applicable conventional grading row that applies to the grading system used by your school to determine a CRS when absolute class rank is not given.)

Percentage Average	Letter Grade Average	11.0 Scale Average	4.0 Scale Average	CRS
98 and above	A+	12.00 and above	4.30 and above	80
97.00–97.99		11.70–11.99	4.20–4.29	79
96.00–96.99		11.40–11.69	4.10–4.19	78
95.00–95.99	A	11.00–11.39	4.00–4.09	77
94.00–94.99		10.70–10.99	3.90–3.99	75
93.00–93.99		10.40–10.69	3.80–3.89	73
92.00–92.99	A−	10.00–10.39	3.70–3.79	71
91.00–91.99		9.80–9.99	3.60–3.69	70
90.00–90.99		9.50–9.79	3.50 -3.59	69
89.00–89.99		9.30–9.49	3.40–3.49	68
88.00–88.99	B+	9.00–9.28	3.30–3.39	67
87.00–87.99		8.70–8.99	3.20–3.29	66
86.00–86.99		8.40–8.69	3.10–3.19	65
85.00–85.99	B	8.00–8.39	3.00–3.09	63
84.00–84.99		7.70–7.99	2.90–2.99	61
83.00–83.99		7.40–7.69	2.80–2.89	59
82.00–82.99	B−	7.00–7.39	2.70–2.79	57
81.00–81.99		6.80–6.99	2.60–2.69	55
80.00–80.99		6.50–6.79	2.50–2.59	53
79.00–79.99		6.30–6.49	2.40–2.49	51
78.00–78.99	C+	6.00–6.29	2.30–2.39	49
77.00–77.99		5.70–5.99	2.20–2.29	48
76.00–76.99		5.40–5.69	2.10–2.19	47
75.00–75.99	C	5.00–5.39	2.00–2.09	46
74.00–74.99		4.70–4.99	1.90–1.99	45
73.00–73.99		4.40–4.69	1.80–1.89	44
72.00–72.99	C−	4.00–4.39	1.70–1.79	42
71.00–71.99		3.80–3.99	1.60–1.69	40
70.00–70.99	D+	3.50–3.79	1.50–1.59	38
Below 70.00	D	Below 3.50	Below 1.50	35

INDEX

Note: A *t* following a page number refers to a table; an *f* refers to a figure.

ABOUT THE AUTHOR

Chuck Hughes is a former senior admissions officer at Harvard College, where he spent five years evaluating thousands of undergraduate applications. He is the founder of Road to College, Inc., a premier college consulting service (*www.roadtocollege.com*), and is also a director of product management for Monster.com. Chuck is a Harvard alumnus and was a member of Harvard's 1989 Ice Hockey NCAA Championship team. He received a master's degree from Boston College and makes his home in Boston, Massachusetts.